For Je (handwritten)

Confessions of
And Other Odd Stories

Enjoy! (handwritten)

J. R. Nakken

J R Nakken (signature)

Confessions of a Martian Schoolgirl is a memoir, a true accounting of the author's years 1940 to 1952. Names, however, have been changed in instances where releases could not be obtained and/or where appropriate.

Author photo by Jaime Laitala

Photo of Martian Schoolgirl emblem used by permission, AOWYN Photography, Seattle, Washington

The Preservation Foundation, Inc.
Nashville, Tennessee

Dedicated with eternal respect and gratitude
to the memory of E. Garner Horton,
the author's first mentor.

Acknowledgments:

I am grateful to Readers Digest Association's Reminisce Magazine for the grand prize in its first inaugural memoir contest, as the prize brought this book to fruition. I am most grateful, though, to the Preservation Foundation, Inc. for republishing the book in a loving and respectful manner.

My utmost gratitude is extended to my ninety-year-old soul mate, Dale Nakken, for his superb meals and endless patience ... notwithstanding some daytime tantrums and long nights at the computer, both before and during the publication process of this book. A writer's significant other experiences much alone time, and his contributions to *Confessions of a Martian Schoolgirl and Other Odd Stories* are immeasurable.

Chapter 1

My grandma thought I was a witch. Born as she was in 1888 and raised by her own superstitious Black Irish grandparents, I guess we can't fault her. I was precocious, precognitive, left-handed and wall-eyed—any one of those attributes denoted a pact with the devil. With four in concert, I wonder that she did not drown me in the musty basement cistern. I was seven years old before I realized that her special sign for me—making a cross of her pointy fingers in front of her and extending it in my direction—was not necessarily a good thing.

Despite this, she was kind to me. Grandma always had a cookie available, and in the fleeting year of 1940–41 when my mother left me with her and The Grandfather, she often curled my long dark hair with a lamp-heated curling iron and patted me as she did so. This process, however, was after she scrubbed the head upon which said hair hung, scrubbing it unmercifully at the rainwater pump. It rather took the joy out of the curls and the patting.

The offending green walleye was mostly unseen that year and in several subsequent years. Round silver-framed spectacles had a half patch of black fiber on the outside of the right lens. The theory was that the lazy eye, made blind since the eyeball which viewed only the peripheral world lay behind the patch, would turn itself toward the light at the end of the tunnel—in this case, the uncovered half of the lens. Perhaps it was the patched glasses or maybe the hours and hours of hand-eye exercises with which I was tortured during the war years, but without surgery, today that eye is not lazy but sweetly indolent.

Osceola, South Dakota, in that time immediately before the second War to End All Wars, was a hamlet of only fifty souls on the flat and endless prairie in the eastern part of the state. Dry-land farming was the sole occupation in the local countryside.

The Odoms lived in a compound across Grandma's back field. Mrs. Ada Odom played the piano in the only church in Osceola. She had a brood of four or five, ranging from teenaged Beverly down to babe in arms Leland. The baby had an all-over case of eczema that looked sore and painful, but it didn't seem to bother the happy baby a bit. Their father was Gil, short for Gilbert, and in childhood's insulation from material facts, I do not know what he "did." He drove away from Osceola in his old car in the morning before I even got up, and he pulled into his long driveway at suppertime each weekday. "You can set your clock by that man," my grandma would say, so often that the words sounded weary as they came from her mouth.

I was aware, however, of what Mr. Engebretson did because he and his family all lived in the section foreman's house. The building was an institutional tan, clapboard two-story that seemed to lean out and over the rail bed. He was the boss of all the workers on Osceola's section of the Great Northern Railroad tracks. Mrs. Engebretson was a nondescript mom-type in a print housedress and apron; she yelled and hugged and pretended not to see Karl and me steal the sugar bowl many afternoons that summer. We dipped the baby rhubarb stalks into it over and over again as we snacked, never once with a thought of this millennium's horror at double- or triple-dipping. Karl was the oldest Engebretson kid at six, and he was the only dark-haired one. Perhaps I cannot remember the names and sexes of the two or three towheads, who were younger than he, because I was buried deep in infatuation. I took off the damned glasses when I went to the Engebretson's, for Karl was my first love.

Yet I nitpicked that first man in my life, a harbinger of years and relationships to come. Karl couldn't read. He would go to school for the first time after harvest, and he'd learn to read there, he said. He could count, but he couldn't read the numbers that flashed by on the sides of the trains. My four-year-old brain

8

couldn't fathom that he not only couldn't unscramble the sounds of the little words that I was already familiar with but also didn't care. I had longed to read words since I first saw my mama reading a magazine, and one day, a few days after my fourth birthday, I just could. It was easy. Grandma crossed her pointy fingers a lot when I asked her, "Is this right?" about a word in the weekly *Iroquois Chief* newspaper, but she always answered me.

The daily train, the Galloping Goose, brought the mail to The Grandpa's post office. Well, actually, it left the mailbag and any parcels at the Great Northern Depot, and the agent held it for him. But sometimes the agent brought it down to the store if he needed a can of Copenhagen or a bottle of pop. Mr. Larson was the father of a really grown-up girl who went to high school in Bancroft or Iroquois, and I never, ever saw his wife. They had the prettiest little white house in all of Osceola, though, with myriad shrubs and flowers in the summertime. It was on the last street (there were only three), behind the opera house.

Ah, yes—the old opera house. Deserted since the Great Crash, which I didn't understand at the time, its lower end was now exclusively Osceola's icehouse. It was around the outhouse and directly across a dusty, overgrown alley from The Grandpa's square, brick general store, where the Osceola post office resided in the far corner. I spent many a fantasy hour alone in its upper half, and Karl and I often sneaked into the section below on a hundred-degree prairie day and lay on the cool, damp straw that insulated the layers of ice.

Grandma was always up early, and one hot summer morning I was watching her slicing bacon with the shiny knife when The Grandpa rushed from their bedroom and headed across the kitchen to the back door and the outhouse. He was wearing only his light cotton nightshirt, and a long, fat finger preceded him, protruding from the gown's short bottom. Grandma flailed the knife at him as he fumbled at the doorknob. "Get rid of that thing before I cut it off," she screamed in a voice I'd never heard before.

"Do you have a fat finger in your underpants?" I asked Karl the next time we sneaked into the icehouse. Turns out, he wasn't wearing any underpants, only cutoff jeans with a frayed bottom, which he shucked in a second. Where his fat finger should have been was a teeny little nub, and I lost all interest in male anatomy right there on the ice, in August of 1940.

Chapter 2

The white schoolhouse with its red roof was directly across Osceola's main gravel road from Grandma's house. Alone in the side yard sat a merry-go-round, an octagon of wooden slab seats set in rusty iron pipes. Karl and I could push it and hop on for a few squeaky circles around the dusty grass, but it was too heavy for me alone, so I didn't go over there by myself. Two freshly painted white outhouses were behind the school, ready for the school year, which began on Tuesday after Labor Day. Grandma wouldn't let me go.

"Karl is going! Karl can't even read, and he is going. *I want to go to school*," I wailed, my four-year-old heart broken. She forbade me to cross the borrow pit, even when the kids were out for recess, so I sat on the porch and watched four or five kids at a time get a really good ride on the merry-go-round due to synchronized pushing, hopping and riding.

The school called to me daily, and I waited a couple of weeks until one morning when Grandma had relaxed her vigilance. I darted across the road after the last bell rang and all the kids were inside, and I crept up the wide concrete steps. When the heavy door's one side creaked open, I was on a square, polished wood floor with two doors on each side. Voices came from the door on my immediate right. I slithered along the right-hand wall ... and bang! There was a long cloakroom with a couple of sweaters on the hangers. At the far end was a kind of screen, maybe an air vent, that went through to the schoolroom. I could hear the counting and the singing, and I had learned to sing, "One and one is two, two and two is four, four and four is ..." before Grandma came and found me. She licked me pretty good, but it was worth it, and I ran away to school every time I could.

It became a game with Mrs. Long, I think. The

11

schoolteacher was really old (today I believe she was, like my ancient grandmother, in her midfifties) and dressed exclusively in black dresses that rustled when she walked. I could hear her coming before her soft voice said, "You go home now, Judy," and she often patted my butt as I passed her in the cloakroom's door.

The whole town and most of the country folks came to the Halloween party at school. The younger kids in the school sang a song in costume, people brought food and homemade ice cream and we had root beer floats.

The room opposite the schoolroom door was where Mrs. Long lived during the week. She drove her black Model A Ford back to Huron and her husband on the weekends. Her room had a big black woodstove and a narrow bed with pillows that made it look almost like a sofa, and it was neat as a pin. I still didn't know what was behind the other two doors, since I knew all the kids were in the one room. "There used to be high school in there," Grandma told me once, "before the crash, when Osceola was bigger." There was that "crash" again. I had looked all around the opera house and had seen no sign of a wreck, but I didn't want to seem ignorant, so I didn't ask.

Grandma invited Mrs. Long to supper on the next Thursday night, and we had stubble duck and pie. I read a little of the newspaper to her and sang as much of the number song as I had learned in my visits to the cloakroom. She went home to the school as soon as the lamps were lit and The Grandpa began to listen to *The Lone Ranger*. I really liked her.

The first week in November smelled like snow, The Grandpa said, and the nippy wind would bring a lot of coats in which to hide in my cloakroom. Grandma made me wash my face and brushed my hair after breakfast on Monday, and then she stayed in the outhouse a really long time, so across the road I scuttled! Mrs. Long caught me before I heard one lesson. But she had a different look on her face and held out her hand. "Come on, Judy. I have a desk for you."

Chapter 3

My two long-held suspicions were verified almost immediately in that one-room repository of knowledge, with prints of Rosa Bonheur's *Horse Fair* and *Old Ironsides* hanging above the side blackboard. With its seventeen kids in grades one through eight, I could learn bigger words and read longer books soon after I went to school, because they were all there on the walls and the shelves and in the big kids' overheard lessons. That was the good suspicion come true. But I learned, irrevocably, that I was not like other kids, and that was the other. It was not because of the hated spectacles or the name "Four Eyes," because that was just mean kids being mean. Inside, I knew I was not the same. I was aghast to discover that my blood ran red and thick when I jammed my hand on a nail in the outhouse door. It was just like Norma Jean's when she fell and cut her forehead. I was not like them, blood or no, and they didn't like me. I was always picked last for everything, and even Karl deserted me for the other first-grader, a redheaded country boy, and he ignored me all during the week.

The Grandpa had been right when he smelled snow. But he hadn't smelled how much snow. On my second Saturday as a schoolgirl—Armistice Day, Grandma called it—we had a blizzard. I guess the whole half of the United States was buried in snow, and Osceola was no exception. In one day's wind and snow, banks drifted so high that The Grandpa had to wait until Gil Odom snowshoed across the field to dig out the back door of our one-story house—he had lowered himself from an upper window to uncover his own family's front steps. With all their kids, I wondered how many chamber pots they had, for our two were really nasty before Grandma could get to the outhouse to empty them. The temperature dropped after the snow to thirty-eight degrees below zero.

The county snowplow didn't get to Osceola until Monday, so we couldn't go to school until Tuesday. I could have gone across the street, as I was to do in a later snowstorm when no other kids showed up, but Mrs. Long was snowbound in Huron. On Tuesday, snowpantsed and mittened, we recessed on the frozen snowbanks with our sleds. It was Thursday before it warmed up enough to make snowballs. Then I stayed in the schoolroom and read my book.

Mrs. Long liked me. She picked out books that I could take across the street and read on the weekends. She didn't tell me to mind my own work when she was doing lessons with the bigger kids, as long as I didn't talk. "You're Teacher's Pet," a scrawny farm girl in the third grade accused as I was going home on a Friday after school with a new book, not quite a baby book, either, under my arm. "She's always acting special to you."

I thought to make a friend, an ally, of her. "She'll loan you extra books, too, Polly," I ventured. "Just ask her. You just have to take good care of them."

Polly's look of incredulity was her only answer and spoke more than words. *What would I want with an* extra *book,* it sneered as she ran to her mother's old car. I retreated into my books and vowed never to come out, until the Saturday of the Bananas.

The Grandpa hadn't unpacked the bananas the Goose had brought on Friday, and I was in the store helping him. They came in blackened, baby-coffin-sized wooden boxes with lids that had to be pried off, and they were packed with paper around them so they wouldn't bruise during shipment. "Stand back, Little Judy," he would always say ... "in case a tarantula jumps out." He often told people that he had heard of a storekeeper being bitten by a spider from a case of bananas, but even in my newness to the world, I wondered about that. It seemed like I could always tell when lies or fibs or stuff they weren't really sure about came out of grown-up mouths.

Soon after The Grandpa lifted the stalk of bananas from the

14

crate and began to separate them into bunches, I was to no longer wonder why I didn't fit in. It was my job to put the paper in the box next to the wood box against the wall. If it was that shredded paper, we just threw it away, but the rumpled newspapers and occasional magazines made good fire-starting material for the giant potbellied stove in the middle of the store. Folding paper, I came upon a crumpled, colorful cover and four attached eight-by-eleven sheets of a magazine, *Amazing Stories*. "Don't read ... fold!" The Grandpa scolded me as he had done in times past. So I saved every yellowed page of *Amazing Stories* as I folded.

Some pages were missing, but I didn't care. We had a pull-down map of the sun and its planets at school, and I knew the big kids' remembering sentence: Many Various Energetic Monkeys Jumped Sideways Under Nut Trees-Pluto. Mercury, Venus, Earth, Mars, Jupiter, Saturn, Uranus, Neptune, and Pluto were the planets in order from the sun. I couldn't decipher all the words in the discarded magazine, but the illustrations told me the truth. Other people lived on other planets, and I was one of them. Surely my own folks, probably from Mars, would be back to get me one day. I was content.

Chapter 4

The first Saturday of the school's Christmas vacation was December 21ˢᵗ. Around the red-hot stove in the store, overalled men with muddy rubber galoshes and barnyard smells steaming from their plaid coats talked excitedly about the war in Europe. Would we "get into it"? Was Old Roosevelt a pacifist? (I was going to have to ask someone what that meant, since Mrs. Long was long gone home to Huron.) I was moping around the canned goods with the feather duster, full of self-pity because school would be closed for two full weeks.

The Grandpa had the coffeepot going—he didn't sell much pop in the wintertime, so he brewed coffee for five cents a cup. With all the free fill-'er-ups he gave out, I wondered if he made any money on it or just enjoyed the company and the conversation. The men all headed home while it was full daylight, but it was dark at six when The Grandpa doused the overhead lamps, locked the heavy door and took my hand. It was about half a city block down to our house. "Look, little girl," he said in his gruff but gentle voice, "see the Northern Lights." Pale green stripes, sometimes a paler blue, danced along the horizon beyond the house. As the dark folded in upon itself, the lights grew brighter and more active. It was all clear to me.

This was why Mama left me here and took Sister with her. She knew my own folks would be here to get me. The heavenly lights seemed to grow closer, and I hurried The Grandpa along the road. "I have to pack my stuff," I told him, frantic. What Earth stuff would I need or use on Mars? I wondered. But I would take my two books, for sure. In the supper-smelling house, Grandma told me to calm down in her no-nonsense voice, hands in apron, black eyes flashing as she shook her head in wonderment. But I couldn't. I kept trying to get outside where they could see me when

16

they got here, but she put me in my bedroom without supper and locked the door. As the green lights flashed, and then faded and disappeared beyond my window shade, I screamed and wept until I slept, alone on Earth.

There was a big snowstorm, or small blizzard, on Monday, and no one got to town for three days except for Santa Claus. I helped Grandma string fresh popcorn, and I clipped most of the candleholders to the right branches on Sunday before the program at church. I said my piece about "Hang up the baby's stocking," and it was long and I did it perfectly, but mostly the people who clapped were whispering to each other.

I didn't care. I really wanted to light the tree candles on Christmas Eve. Grandma wouldn't. She was too afraid of fire, she said, but she kept the "one candle for baby Jesus" lit in the window all night. Santa Claus left me the Sandy Squirrel book and a warm new red dress. How good it looked with my long dark curls, my grandma said. I didn't think so. For the first time, I wondered if there were others like me on Earth, and if Santa Claus knew all of them, too. I stayed in my room most of the time until school took up again. At night, I watched the northern sky.

17

Chapter 5

Recess was not outside in the subzero prairie mornings, and not often in the afternoons. We were free to quietly (*quietly*) pursue individual activities, Mrs. Long said. On occasion, she would start a game of Alphabet Geography or Simon Says. The *A*'s were valuable and about used up in the geography game when I answered my fourth-grade cousin, Gale's, "California" with "Aruba."

"No such thing as 'Aruba,'" one of the big girls complained, next to play off the last letter or forfeit. "Mrs. Long, that little snot cheats." I knew there was such a place because I saw it in the *A–B* volume of the encyclopedia, dusty on a back shelf. But in the same breath, I knew that Mrs. Long wasn't sure.

"We'll just check to be fair," she said and saved her face as she went to the back of the room and returned with that same *A–B* volume. Vindicated, I remained quiet. Martian kids were smarter than Earth teachers, was the lesson I learned that day.

The hard freeze didn't thaw, and it was soon time for the ice harvest. There was a big sign in the store window: "Ice Harvest Saturday 7 AM, Sunday if Necessary. Come to Work If You Want to Use It." The sign was yellowed and the letters were faded, as if it had announced this harvest since the beginning of time. Grandpa rang up Central on the phone and told her to tell everyone on the line. He was excused from the work because he had to keep the store open, and because he supplied coffee and sandwich stuff for the workers. I went to Lake Osceola with Grandma that first morning; she took coffee in jars and warm cinnamon rolls. I was almost scared at what they were doing out there in the middle of the lake.

Teams of huge horses, recently retired to their pastures by red International or green John Deere tractors, pranced about the ice, their eager neighs telling one another how glad they were to have work to do. Aunt Loie's Doc and Don looked practically gleeful. The teams pulled great stone boats, wooden sleds ordinarily used in the fields to pick up stones that would damage the plow blades. Here they would carry their icy load through the snow for two miles to the old opera house. Six pairs of men were on crosscut saws, carving the blocks of ice out of the lake! Other men stood around with iron tongs to lift the two-by-three blocks, cut to fit all the iceboxes in the surrounding community, onto the stone boats.

Lake Osceola wasn't that big—it was a WPA work project in the Great Depression, The Grandpa said—and I was afraid there wouldn't be any water left for swimming come next summer! *Maybe I don't care,* I thought, since I hadn't learned to swim this summer with the other kids. I had decided that Martians did not care to swim.

At the time of the Labor Day picnic, the icehouse had been a shadow of its former self, with blocks of ice in just one corner. The pungent smell of damp straw wasn't pleasant anymore; the ice was melting, and the odor was more like wet dog. But I slogged my way out the store's back door on the next Saturday after the ice harvest, just to check. Yes, it was full to the brim again, with fresh straw between the layers. And I realized while standing there that this place was important to all the people who lived around us, and it wasn't a playhouse. I wasn't going to sneak in there next summer.

In retrospect, I believe Mrs. Long was an early and unsung feminist. In my adult fantasies, there was no Mr. Long in Huron at all, only a house full of books and a cat or two. In that first-grade year, I eavesdropped as much about Rosa Bonheur, Molly Pitcher and Florence Nightingale as I learned about George Washington, Ben Franklin and Honest Abe Lincoln. "Imagine young Rosa," Teacher told the seventh- and eighth-grade class of three, "expelled from all the schools girls were allowed to go to in the 1800s and with no admission of females to the art schools." She pointed to the horses in our two-by-three print of Bonheur's most famous painting and exhorted, "Smell them! Hear their breaths. This is Realism at its finest."

Molly Pitcher, I learned, went right to the battlefield with George Washington when we fought the British for our freedom, and she carried water to cool the cannon barrels so they wouldn't blow up. And Florence Nightingale was in some other war (Crimean) I had never heard of, nursing and doing doctor stuff. You could tell that Mrs. Long was proud of those women.

Teacher played the big black piano that stood on the right side of her desk, and she accompanied the singing. I think she liked singing a lot, because we did it every day, sometimes twice a day. We sang "Solomon Levi" and "A Spanish Cavalier" alone, and then together. It was amazing how the two pieces, so different, blended together when we kept in time with the music. The boys were supposed to do the Solomon Levi part, but they didn't sing loud enough, so a couple of big girls helped them out. We learned "My Country 'Tis of Thee," "Camptown Races," "Beautiful Dreamer," and to say the Pledge of Allegiance to the American flag with our right hands over our hearts and no mention of God.

I thought about Mama a lot when we were singing; she played the piano, I was pretty sure, and not pounding like Mrs. Long, but tinkly and sweet. I wondered if I would ever see her again.

Chapter 6

Winter passed with nothing exciting after Christmas, except the bad burn on my arm from blundering into the red-hot stove at the store. Grandma put a smelly poultice on it and it healed without puckering up, but the long arrowhead-looking scar was on the top of my left arm from the wrist halfway to the elbow. Now I could tell left from right, anyway, something I always had had trouble with. Spring came with torrential downpours that washed out many fields of fragile wheat; those farmers who were able to, replanted. Mrs. Long went away on a Friday in the end of May, promising to return after Labor Day. I passed the first grade, and The Grandpa was proud of my report card. My pretty aunt Helen had a baby boy, Randy, the day before the Fourth of July picnic, and I got to see him at Aunt Ev's at harvest.

Harvest! Do you know what I liked best about harvest? Oh, it was fun to watch the threshing machine work—it was hooked to a big green John Deere tractor that replaced the horses that had powered it just a couple of years ago. Men and boys with pitchforks balanced themselves on top of wagons filled with shocks of grain. Those shocks had been standing for days in the stubble fields like small tepees, peopled only with nests of field mice. The pitchforks fed the one end of the thresher with those bundles of wheat or oats, and the grain separated from the stalk, a steady stream flowing out of the other end. The straw blew fast and noisy out of a tall smokestack and made a giant haystack in no time. When a wagon was full of grain, it went to be dumped into the farm's tall granary for use as winter feed and spring seed. Or it went on the road to Osceola to be sold to the giant Peavey elevators there, just across the tracks from the Great Northern Depot.

Oh, yes. What I liked best. The food. All the farmers'

neighbors worked at each other's threshing, and all the wives brought food for dinner at noon. Women and children ate in the wallpapered farmhouse kitchen and sitting room, while the males sat in a semicircle in the front yard. They had all splashed some water on their faces and hands at the outside pump before going into the house briefly to load up their plates. Stuffed chicken and pheasant-called-stubble-duck, roasted beef, hot bread and pickles, jam and canned vegetables from their gardens were the main meal; the serving dishes covered the whole expanse of Aunt Ev's square oak dining table. Then there were the pies on the kitchen table—apple, pumpkin, peach and my favorite, sour cream raisin. Grandma cooked very well—don't get me wrong—and we had pie a lot. But there were just the three of us, so I had never seen ... so much food.

Tony and Alfonso didn't speak English, and I didn't quite understand how they had come from Mexico to be helping Osceola farmers with harvest. Grandma said she would tell me when I was older, but I guess she died too soon, because I never did find out. I thought maybe Alfonso was Tony's dad ... anyway, he was a lot older. They each had a neat bundle that must have contained clean clothes and maybe a blanket, for they slept in the barn at night when the neighbors went home. Both days that I spent at Aunt Ev's, being pestered by little cousin Gene and tormented by his big brother, Gale, Tony played his guitar and sang by lantern light in the yard after supper. His singing was as sweet as the round black records Auntie Helen played on her gramophone, even if none of us could understand a word of it. I wondered if Martian would sound like Mexican, and if I would understand it when I needed to.

"The luck of the draw" was the talk in the store after the hailstorm. Threshing was nearly over, with only one more farm's harvest to complete, when the sky blackened and the heavens opened in the space of ten minutes. Baseball-sized ice fell for another ten minutes, flattening anything left in the fields and denting cars, roofs and slow people indiscriminately.

The farmer who had drawn the last lot in the threshing rotation had hail insurance, which not all of the neighbors had purchased. "How lucky it was him," they said. Then they gossiped about how that neighbor, seeing his wheat only 70 percent destroyed, borrowed another tractor, and he and his grown son and a long length of chain made sure the claim would be 100 percent paid. They bragged on it. It didn't sound fair to me.

Chapter 7

They came in the round green '39 Ford, not as shiny as when they brought me, and took me away from Osceola when the summer was over. Mama hugged me and called me her big girl, and Sister snuggled under my arm on the scratchy backseat. Father Wessman, whom I really didn't know yet, was square-jawed with gray hairs around his ears. He was about as old as The Grandpa, I thought, and he didn't talk much. "Took good care of those glasses, I see," was about all he said to me. "We gotta go," he told Grandma. "It's a long way to North Bend, Nebraska."

It was. It was forever away. We lived in a dark apartment in the basement of a big old house, and the lady upstairs did not like noise. Some days, when Mama didn't have a headache, we would go to the park, where Sister and I could swing and play on the monkey bars. I endured everything because it was just a few days until school started.

I could not understand when they said, "This is Nebraska. We have guidelines," in the wood-paneled and paper-strewn school office, which smelled like Mama's Lysol. But I was pretty sure I knew what "no exceptions" meant, when Mama took me to school the first day. It was just up the hill from our house, and I could have gone by myself, but I soon knew why she accompanied me. I had just turned five years old, and the guidelines said I had to go to kindergarten. Kindergarten! Kindergarten was where thirty baby kids colored balloons outside the lines and didn't even know what the printed numbers were inside the balloons. Kindergarten was eating graham crackers and milk and nap time and where only the teacher read books. I skipped school for the first time, the first of many, in kindergarten in North Bend, Nebraska.

The rest of my time at North Bend is a blur. There was war that winter, and I was untouched. We moved to a real house the

24

next year. I went to the first grade for the second time, where others were just learning to read and had never heard of Florence Nightingale or Rosa Bonheur. Father Wessman was not there when Sister and I got up one October morning, and he stomped breathless through red and dying leaves onto the porch moments later. "Your mother had a baby boy last night," he announced in a voice I had never heard—an almost nice voice. I can recall no previous knowledge or curiosity about the little brother's origin; I accepted it with the apathy that began when my own folks didn't find me back there in Osceola to take me home to Mars. The apathy was cemented forever when I had to go to kindergarten. Father took us to see Mama in a big house with a bunch of beds, and mothers and babies all around. Baby Keith Brooks, forever "Keeto," was sleeping but looked too pretty to be a boy. Father seemed to be happier after the baby came, and he didn't whip me nearly as often as he used to.

Father got war work. He was "rolling in clover," I heard him tell our neighbor, and we moved to Morse Bluff that summer to be closer to his work, since you couldn't get a lot of gas for the green Ford anymore. It was a village only about three times the size of Osceola, and we had a big, big house but used only the bottom floor. Sliding doors went from the hallway to the parlor, which was the twin bedroom for Sister Nancy and me. Keeto slept in his crib in Mama's room.

Every kid in Morse Bluff, Nebraska, spoke Bohemian. Those who had been to school could talk English, too, but they didn't when I was around, except for Jessie Ann. She was eight and lived in the section house next door. It leaned over the railroad track just like the Engebretsons' in Osceola, and it was the same ugly old color, too. She was always busy taking care of her little brothers and sisters, so I spent the rest of the summer exploring the new surroundings. On the edge of town was Indian Peak. Even in my seven-year-old eyes, it wasn't a peak ... just a gentle hill and easy to climb through the underbrush to its top. Jessie Ann said there was a marker for a dead Indian at the top, but I never could find it. I took mulberries and pears from the trees at our new house and pretended that I was lost in the wilderness, eating what berries and stuff I could scavenge. The Morse Bluff school—a two-story brick building with the grade school on the first floor and the high school on the second—was once again just up the hill from our house. And that office seemingly had not heard of Nebraska's guidelines! Sister started first grade when she had just been five in June, and the nice woman behind the counter told Mama that the second-grade teacher would "assess Judy as to proper placement." What that meant was that I was in third grade before Halloween, and I was supposed to be in fourth grade when the New Year of 1944 rang in, but we moved during Christmas vacation. Oh, how I loved the thought of being out of the room that held grades one through three. There were three reasons for that: (1) little sister Nancy (2) Wade Bell and (3) lots of books in the next highest room!

Wade Bell? He and his family moved to Morse Bluff shortly after we did, and Father and Wade's dad often rode to work together to save gas. Finally, I thought at first, there was another American family in this village of foreign-speakers ... and then school started and I learned to think better thoughts about the Bohemian locals. Wade's hands were always dirty, and he smudged everything he touched. But mostly, he had my name in the Christmas drawing, and I knew beforehand that I would not have a present under the tree—the only one at the whole school program with no gift. I hated him and tried to put the Martian evil eye on him, but he didn't die.

I was probably the only one whose mother didn't come to the program, too. She always said she would try, but she didn't try very hard, because she never came. She lied about a lot of other things, too, little things that shouldn't have been important enough to lie about. I learned, at six or seven, not to believe a word she said.

26

Before autumn, when there were leaves to hide me, I spent a lot of time with my book up in the pear tree in front of the house. With the sheltering leaves still moldering in piles on what passed for a lawn and spring just bursting, I looked for a new hiding place. A vacant piece of property adjoined the school yard. There was a high fence on the school side and across the front, but just bushes and trees secreted it from the rest of the town on the other two sides. I was reading *Girl of the Limberlost* that May when I discovered it. My path bent bushes and saplings that snapped right back into place, and I was alone and hidden in a foreign landscape. The book and the non-Martian surroundings were my reality when I wasn't in school, and now, at nearly eight, I began to suspect deep in my old soul that my Martian heritage was probably only a fantasy. But I clung to it, nonetheless, for there was nothing else to sustain me.

Chapter 8

Watertown, South Dakota, was next, for the last half of the third grade and all of the fourth grade. Across the street was a hospital where Little Sister's life was saved from a ruptured appendix. Father Wessman was done with war work, even though the war wasn't over; Mama drove him to his new work on Monday morning, and he came home only on the weekends. Mama had a piano again, and she whirled on the piano stool and sang the hit songs of the day. She was often not home when Father got home on Friday nights, and that's when he was the meanest—only to me, of course. It got worse when Daddy Bud came to see me.

I didn't know about the divorce, which had happened when I was barely two and Sister was a newborn, but there had been cards for my last two birthdays, so I was aware of a "real dad" somewhere on the planet. On this day, Mama took both Nancy and me downtown and parked the car, and we walked toward the bus station. She walked right past the bulky man lounging in the doorway, but I pulled away and ran back to him. I remembered! I remembered his lap and soda pop. Nancy was shy and didn't want to go with him, but I did. We went and had a horse-meat hamburger (beef was abroad with our brave soldiers, the sign said) and a Coca Cola, and he gave me one of the packages he carried. It was a pair of roller skates! It was nearly impossible to get roller skates in 1944, all metal with metal clamps to tighten onto your shoes, and these were not new, but, oh, I was the darling of the sidewalks in my part of town. Mama came back to the bus station to get me, and Nancy got a pretty little doll.

I wouldn't see him again for another three years.

Old Roosevelt died that next spring. The announcement interrupted my after-school radio program, *Jack Armstrong, the All-American Boy.* I ran upstairs. "Mama! President Roosevelt just died!"

She dropped the box of bobby pins, and her beautiful face was witchy as she smacked mine. "Bad girl! Bad, ugly girl! Never, never say such a thing." I knew she would find out for herself, so I retreated down the stairs because she hardly ever hit me. Jack Armstrong was over when I got back to my rug in front of the radio, though.

Mama cried a lot the next few days, and she drank a lot more of the whiskey than she usually did. I missed her piano playing.

The mom-and-pop grocery store on that Watertown corner redeemed pop bottles—three cents apiece or two for a nickel. An ice cream cone was a nickel, and seven pop bottles would earn me an extra treat if I redeemed them one at a time! It went on for a couple of weeks, my scavenging for the bottles—which most often were available out there on the edge of town on Sunday morning— and taking them, one at a time, for the three-cent refund. It was the missus who came down hard on my scheme. "You bring those bottles in two at a time, little missy, or take them someplace else!" When I got my next butter-pecan ice cream cone for five pennies, I looked at it and wondered how many pennies it cost the mister to make it. I decided it cost three cents to make it and he got to keep only two cents, and that was probably why his wife was so chintzy about the pop bottles.

I took some piano lessons that year. I was a "natural," the teacher told my mama. I wanted to play the violin, and she told Mama I was ready to do so, but I would have to have the instrument restrung in order to bow with my dominant left hand. Father put his foot down. First of all, he wasn't going to buy a violin with a piano already in the house. And secondly, if he ever did, I could play it right-handed. I wondered a lot about that, since he was left-handed himself.

Father had no work, and the longer it went on, the meaner he got. He whipped me with belts, yardsticks and whatever was

29

handy, for sins both real and imagined. The missus at the grocery store saw the purple-and-green bruises on my legs one day when I was taking in my two pop bottles. "They ought to do something about that man," she raged to the mister behind the cash register. But "they," whoever "they" were, didn't do anything.

"I want to go back to Osceola," I told him and Mama at breakfast one day when he was trying to make me sick to my weak stomach by telling me how dirty the pigs were that bacon came from. "Grandpa needs me in the store, anyway." Father agreed that it was a grand idea and said he would go pack a suitcase for me. In minutes, he and Mama had me loaded into the Ford and drove me onto a country road on the edge of Watertown.

"Osceola is that way," he said, and he pointed down the road as he set the scuffed little tan suitcase in the warm gravel. Sister's big eyes in the round rear window were the last things I saw as the car turned around and headed back toward town.

I dragged the suitcase only fifty steps or so. How could my clothes be so heavy? Opened, the suitcase disclosed nothing but a few bricks insulated by an old brown towel. I was only eight, but it was clear that Father was teaching me a lesson, that no one ever expected me to walk to Osceola. I left the suitcase there on the road and walked another half mile while I decided what to do. They would be back for me before long, I reasoned, so I cut across a field to a little pond surrounded by underbrush and lay back to watch the road.

Sure enough, here came the Ford. It went up the road past me for a ways and then back down, and I could see it stop, a green speck in the gravel dust at the probable spot where I had abandoned the suitcase and its load. Then it continued back toward town. *They think I'm on my way home,* I thought. So I got my bearings and figured out where the heart of Watertown was, and I angled across fields and under fences until—sure enough—there it was. The street was the one with the ice cream parlor that Mama had taken me and Nancy to a couple of times. I had a nickel, so in I went, surrounded immediately by the cool smell of dairy products on the edge. The clock on the white wall said four o'clock. I had been on my own for six hours and was doing all right so far!

I had a vision or a feeling of Mama—frantic and searching for me along the country road. I started to care a little bit, but then I hardened my heart. *She shouldn't let him be so mean to me,* I thought. Mothers in all the books protected their children. So I went about the business of turning the lesson tables on them, skulking about the Watertown streets until dusk. *Andy Hardy's Double Life* was playing at the movie theater, the signs said, and something about *The Magnificent Ambersons* was coming next. It didn't look very good.

I walked in the front door of my house just as it got dark. It was easy; I just asked a man on the street which way to the hospital. Something in me had changed during the day on my own; I was tall and strong with 20-20 vision and didn't care anymore. Mama actually cried as she hugged me; then she sent me to bed but brought me some milk and a sandwich. Father didn't say a word. I never again saw that little tan suitcase.

Keeto toddled and walked and then ran, and he was hard to keep up with in the year the war ended. Father was home almost all the time during Keeto's third birthday month, and I heard him tell the man that always came for the house money that there was no work for a middle-aged guy with all the boys coming home from Europe. Anyway, one day we packed up the Ford and a little trailer and went to Osceola. I don't know what happened to Mama's piano with the whirly stool.

Chapter 9

Grandma was gone to heaven, they said. I wasn't too sure about the place called heaven, but even with her gone to wherever, the little square two-bedroom house was too crowded for the five of us and The Grandpa. Somehow we made do, although I don't know where The Grandpa slept—surely not in the basement? Mama and Father had the other bedroom, and we three kids slept in the room that used to be mine, where I had wailed at the north window in a time long past. Karl was now two grades behind me; I was bigger than he was, and he still couldn't read very well. I spent a lot of time in the store, clerking now because I could add columns of figures. Grandpa bragged on me and also ordered books for me to read. They came in the mail all the way from the Traveling Library in Pierre, the state capitol. One day he brought home a Coleman lantern, for the REA had not yet brought power to this part of eastern South Dakota, and it made the night like day compared to the kerosene lamps. "Now you can read at night, too," he told me, "until the darned Rural Electrification gets here."

I heard him talking about Father to the men around the stove. "He's a worker, he is. Not a bit lazy. Just having a bit of hard luck, that's all." And it was true—no matter how he treated me, and I don't call him "my wicked stepfather" for no reason—I have to admit he was always busy. He dug a well at Grandpa's house … now we didn't have to carry drinking water from the store as we had always done, as the rainwater cistern was only for dishwashing and bathing. Then he wired Aunt Ev's and Aunt Loie's houses for electricity powered with Delco plant generators, then the store, and then Grandpa's house! "Wish he was a plumber, too," The Grandpa chuckled to his cronies. "We could sure use a bathroom. Don't know where we'd put it, though."

I spent my solitary time in the old opera house, no dustier

32

above than it had been when I was four and five. The black grand piano still leaned drunkenly at the edge of a ramshackle stage, with bird droppings along the wall. Some of the hooked-together wooden seats were gone, I thought, but the piano bench was still there. I spent hours trying to coax a little music out of the rusty keys. One day I got the bright idea to give my mama all the ivory —surely it was worth a lot of money, and she could get a new dress or something. I pried off all the white "ivories" that still existed and took them home one day. "Oh, Judy, don't be silly." My mama laughed and threw a kitchen match into the pile of celluloid on the back grass.

I dreamed about the Sunday drowning at Lake Osceola on the previous Friday night. I knew beforehand that Uncle Charl was going to be fired from the RFD mail delivery job he'd had "since Tige was a pup," and I knew the little girl was hiding something when she and her mother came to the front door. "Where is the doll?" were the first words out of my mouth. It turns out this was Daddy Bud's sister and her only child, a spoiled seven-year-old, and Aunt Bobbie had told little Julie Ann to leave the new doll in the car because we might not have anything so nice ... or some such nonsense.

I heard my mama. "She's always been that way, Bobbie. She just knows things. It gets real scary." Then she added, "And in other ways, she's dumber than dirt!" *Still thinking about the ivory,* I figured.

The war was over the summer that I was nine. My glasses had plastic frames now, with a prism in the right lens instead of the black patch. I passed into the sixth grade. Although I really liked Osceola and The Grandpa, I hoped Father would get a job in some other town before September; I had read everything in Mrs. Long's schoolroom, encyclopedias included.

I was swinging Keeto around by his arms one Sunday when a lot of the aunts and uncles were at The Grandfather's house. He was giggling his baby head off when his giggle became a yelp, he

33

pawed at his right shoulder and began to scream. Everyone came running. The three-year-old's right arm hung strangely from his shoulder. "What did you do?" Mama asked as Father was urging people to move their cars at the top of his lungs so he could take Keeto to the doctor in Iroquois. I didn't think I did anything, I told her. I was just swinging him like I had been doing forever. She ran to the car to comfort her baby boy while I sat alone on the back porch, shivering. He came soon and tapped on my shoulder, and I looked up into eyes of pure hatred. "If his arm is broken, I will kill you," he promised in a steel monotone, and he whirled away.

I knew that he would. What could I do? Could I run away? No—if I left on foot, he would be sure to catch me. I decided The Grandpa would protect me, for he had once told Father, "Don't you think that's enough, Wes?" when I was getting a hard whipping. After all the aunts and uncles and cousins were gone, Grandpa told me not to worry and sent Nancy and me to our room. I heard his raised voice when they got home. "My house!" was repeated several times. Mama brought Keeto to his crib, and his arm was in a sling but just sprained from its socket. He would be fine in no time. Father never mentioned it again, and Keeto still loved me.

Chapter 10

I could be a help to Aunt Ev, she said, and I spent the whole week of threshing at her house. She really liked me, I knew, even though she didn't hug and kiss or really say so. I thought it was probably because she was different from her other three sisters, too, and I began to entertain a theory that the oldest, if not a Martian, was always unlike the rest of the siblings. She had black hair and black eyes like Grandma, while my mama was auburn and Helen and Loie were fair. But the difference was lots more than looks; Evelyn had skinny black chickens, while every other farmwife in the countryside kept fat white hens. She wouldn't have a nasty telephone in her house, and she wore black or navy blue slacks at all times, even to church. I could feel that she adored her youngest, my cousin Gene, who was a year younger than I, but it didn't look like he got hugs or kisses, either. She did ruffle his hair and venture a seldom-seen smile, however, and when she smiled I realized that she was as pretty as my beautiful mother. "Pep," she called him, after his favorite cereal, and she would smile again. "Aw, g'wan now," she'd say when she stopped smiling.

Really, all I did was wash and dry dishes—lots of dishes—and feed the chickens. The rest of the time I was free to wander about the farm or go into the near pasture to watch the threshing. The shock-tepees in the stubble fields were made of five or six bundles of grain, stacked like an inverted cone in rows all along the field. The placement of the grain bundles, the shocks, was so that the water would drain down and off if it rained in the time between the cutting and baling of the shocks and the threshing itself. Men on the ground in those stubble fields forked the bundles onto the horse- or tractor-drawn wagons to send back to the threshing machine.

In almost all of the tepees, nests of mice were uncovered.

The mamas often got away, but the pitchforks speared as many of young and old alike as they could reach. And there were many little pink-and-gray babies. I rescued four of them and took them, hidden, home to my one dresser drawer. I tried to feed them with Sister's doll bottle, but they all died. I buried them, but I didn't cry.

School took up again soon after harvest. I couldn't skip school in Osceola, with Father right across the street most of the time … but oh, I wanted to! I had already learned the sixth-grade lessons and whatever else was going on in the room, and there was nothing to read … no new pictures or posters on the walls. I guess I wandered around too much, and Mrs. Long didn't like me as well as she had when I was little. Karl, the only boyfriend material for me in Osceola, quit me for a cute little blond first-grader because she kissed better than I did. And when school let out in May, I knew I could not go back to the seventh grade in that room. If push came to shove, I would really run away.

Chapter 11

I didn't have to make a decision, for that summer Father got his last job and we moved to Iroquois, a big town of about three hundred souls a few miles down the county line road from Osceola and The Grandpa. Father was the representative of the electric company, Northwestern Public Service, for that and several little towns in the area. He read meters, did repair work and often went out in storms with his heavy climbing boots slung over his shoulder. We bought an old house (I think The Grandfather helped with that) with four bedrooms upstairs and one down, a little root cellar and an outhouse. The first year our heat was a coal stove in the large dining room downstairs; the heat went up a chimney and warmed the big middle room upstairs. All three of us slept in that room in the winter.

I got breasts. They were little bumps for about twenty minutes, and then they grew and grew and grew, until Father wondered out loud why I didn't fall over on my face. I menstruated for the first time in that summer of 1946 and about once a year thereafter due to a condition that would be discovered in adulthood, Stein-Leventhal syndrome. As part of cosmic balance, I guess, precognition left me about the same time, except for brief glimpses in succeeding years, and I always blamed the breasts and the blood.

I was the new girl in Miss Ramsell's seventh- and eighth-grade classroom, and though a couple of years younger, I was as mature as anyone there. I learned "Casey at the Bat" for a program with all its umpteen verses, and Mama said she would come, but she didn't. I had quit looking for her several years before, anyway. But I could check out books in the high school library upstairs, so I didn't care once more.

Seventh grade was a blur, what with getting used to the

new house and Father digging a basement, installing a furnace and making a bathroom in the bedroom at the top of the stairs. A nice bathroom, it had a stool and an enclosed tub and sink with a medicine chest above it. What it didn't have was a door. I do not remember Father ever barging in on anyone in the bathroom, though, and the expectation of no privacy on the john or in the bathtub was just another part of the twisted family dynamic.

As was suppertime. Sending me upstairs to the no-door bathroom to vomit was the grand finale of his day, and more days than not he had his way with me. Escaping into a book calmed my stomach, but he soon forbade reading at the table. In retrospect, I wonder that I didn't get bulimia or anorexia or another eating disorder.

The Iroquois school building was a carbon copy of the one at Morse Bluff—square, red brick with a big round tube of a fire escape snaking down its whole right side. High school was upstairs, four rooms for grade school were downstairs, and the high schoolers took typing in a room in the basement. The gymnasium was a block down the street, and was really the Roman Catholic Church's auditorium. All school functions—dances, programs and basketball games—took place there. The painted cement floor had a tendency to sweat in the wintertime, and visiting basketball teams complained of the slipping and sliding. I think our guys were used to it, and that's why they won so much.

There were no friends, but I was used to that. The boys in this hamlet, where every schoolkid had a nickname, called me "Brain." (The next year, after I slipped on the ice and was on crutches for weeks, they switched to "Gimp.") The Catholic priest, who had served in Iroquois for many years, came to visit my mother a couple of times a year. Eavesdropping, I learned that this was the little town where my sister had been born and where I remembered the Daddy Bud lap and the soda pop, and that we girls were "baptized Catholics." Nothing ever came of it, though, because Father insisted that we go to the Protestant Methodist

Sunday school.

I was pretty sure I didn't believe in this loving God, and I didn't want to go to the classes for joining the church. "I'm too young," I told him. "You have to be twelve." They had made a special dispensation for me, he said, and I was going. Mrs. Stevenson, the preacher's wife, had an English accent and believed vocally in the everlasting love of God. Eleanor was there, and she was the classmate who had always been the most kind to me. I broke my self-imposed rule and talked to her. "Doody, do you believe in God?"

"You'll go to hell, Judy Roberts!" she whispered at the top of her lungs, and she moved as far away from me as she could get on the bench in the cold church classroom. I ate all the bitter foxglove leaves on the tiny plants the night before the church induction, though, and I was so sick during the night that my mama nearly called the doctor. I didn't have to join the church, and no one ever told me to do so again.

May-Basket Day came. I don't think we had it in Watertown, nor in Osceola. It was a big deal in Iroquois, South Dakota, and my mama knew it. From somewhere in her artsy supplies, she materialized crepe paper and pipe cleaners, and Nancy and I made May baskets on the usually unused dining room table. Tiny boxes became colorful receptacles for a few pieces of candy, the nicer pieces for someone you really liked. On May 1st, you sneaked around to kids' homes, placed the basket, knocked and ran away. How fast you ran depended on who got the box, for if they caught you, they kissed you. I didn't get kissed for the three boxes Mama forced me to make and deliver—one was to Eleanor, anyway, and she probably wouldn't have caught me.

Edna May Hoevet (she billed herself with all three names) was the wife of the local undertaker. The mortuary was directly across a side street from the big Methodist edifice. It had family living quarters in one end, even a tiny, picket-fenced backyard for her two little boys to play in. She was big and loud, wore many

39

hats on hair always askew, and played the piano in her own Voice. Mama took me on an early Saturday afternoon to talk about piano lessons.

Mrs. Hoevet played the first part of Grieg's "March of the Dwarfs" to indicate her proficiency, and I was sold. She was so wild, so free at the piano, and I wanted to be her. But the music lessons were fifty cents. "I'll have to talk to my husband," Mama said, and I knew what that meant. No, that's what it meant.

"I could babysit," I said. "So you won't have to take two little kids when you go downtown." We struck a bargain, and for the next three years, I played with Billy and Bobby and scrubbed her tiny kitchen floor on Saturday afternoons. We had our music lesson when she returned from shopping, and I was delighted with the exchange as, I am sure, was she.

I got a paper route, too. It was the daily—*The Huronite and Daily Plainsman*—and two little girls delivered the few papers north of the highway after I took them up there every night. I had about forty houses in Iroquois proper. Now I had a few dollars' a month spending money and was in hog heaven. On Saturdays about once a month, Aunt Ev would take me to Huron with her. I spent all my money on magazines, only occasionally on a new pair of bobby socks, while she and Gene went to the movies. Occasionally she would treat me to the movie with them. Mama wouldn't let me go to see *Duel in the Sun*, though. "She's at that age," is all she told her sister. "Better if she doesn't go." I didn't get it. Gene was a year younger, and he got to see it.

Flying saucers abounded in the South Dakota skies all summer long. I buried my nose in whatever I was reading and, at eleven, tried not to succumb to the probable fantasies of my childhood.

Chapter 12

Eighth grade was a mélange of accolade and agony. Homecoming was in October, and each room downstairs and each class upstairs sold tickets for their chosen prince and princess, king and queen. Tickets were ten cents, three for a quarter, and we sold them for just ten days. The room or class that brought in the most money would crown their selected pair. Every year in recorded memory, the senior high school pair and the little kids from the first- and second-grade room wore the crowns. Keeto was in little kids' room, and I hoped he'd be chosen as their prince candidate.

Clare Sorheim nominated me for princess, amid stifled snorts and giggles. I snapped out of my reverie at the sound of my name. Why? I didn't get it. He really disliked me, because he was half-smart and my test scores messed everything up, he said, when they were graded on a curve. Miss Ramsell had to insist on another nomination. When the other girl and I returned to the room after the voting, Judy Roberts had won by a landslide.

It didn't take me long to "get it." Another boy nominated Duane, called "Monk," a fifteen-year-old seventh-grader with reddened eyes and green teeth. Monk won the vote in a landslide, and he and I were our room's candidates. It was a giant practical joke on me, perpetrated by the whole class. *Not to worry,* I thought. *The little kids will win.*

Upsets occurred, upstairs and down. Miss Ramsell's room sold more tickets than ever before, as did the junior class in the high school. I had to reign over the homecoming festivities with my prince, Monk. I have to admit, he was scrubbed up and tooth-shiny for the ordeal, and he went through the ritual paces with me with what Mrs. Schultz called "grace and dignity." He totally ignored the halfhearted catcalls that came from a few teenaged voices as he took my arm for the promenade.

When we were seated and reigning, Monk's mother came to the stage. How like him she was, with reddened eyes that threatened to spill over. "You did so good, son, just like I told you, and I am so proud of you ..." She wanted to hug and kiss him but didn't, and she melted away into the crowded gymnasium.

"My mama didn't tell me anything, Monk. What did yours say?"

He stammered and reverted to tongue-tied Monk, but he finally blurted it out. "This has really been all right, Judy, and you are, too. My mom told me that no matter if it was a joke on me, I was to treat you like a princess."

Darlene and Eleanor asked me to do cheerleader tryouts with them because it had to be a threesome and probably all the other girls were booked. I had no desire to be an eighth-grade cheerleader and go to the basketball games with the jocks, but I wanted to be friends with Darlene—she of the mature coloratura soprano voice and really nice clothes—so I said I would. Bad idea. It seemed that the boys liked the idea of my huge breasts bouncing up and down in the course of the cheerleading job. And then the vote was for singles, and Darlene didn't make it. Eleanor and I and a pretty seventh-grader named Shirley were chosen, and I bounced around for one whole season and hated every minute of it. Aunt Ev bought me my orange school sweater, and it cost fifty cents to have it cleaned. I grew well aware of that fact, for if I left it lying around, Father would throw it down the dirty-clothes chute, where his stinking work clothes piled up until wash day. Ugh.

That winter after basketball, the treacherous South Dakota ice-under-snow on the school steps caused a cracked bone in my left leg. My mama always told me to wear clean underwear in case I was in an accident, but she never said anything about white bobby socks. I had only two pair—one to wash and one to wear—and I had not washed socks for several days when one of the big high school boys drove me downtown to the doctor. He was right there when Dr. Heilsen took off my shoe and exposed my not-so-clean white sock. I wanted to yell, "My underpants are perfect!" but didn't. I just retreated into my I-don't-care place. Father took my crutches away from me when my leg still hurt and wouldn't let me take a ride if it was offered on the half-mile walk to school or church, earning him the title of Meanest Man in Town.

When I won a big spelling bee, I was the toast of the town for fifteen minutes. Visions of accepting the plaque from President Truman when I won the national contest danced in my head, for I could spell every big word in the dictionary. I returned from the Regional after the first round, shaking my head and retreating even further into my books and fantasy. There is no *a* in *cemetery*, a really small word.

Ernest W. Lunn was the school principal, presiding over us, brown-suited and armpit-stained, in the office at the head of the wide stairs. Behind him on the wall was a rubber-coated paddle, which I think was probably a table tennis paddle now that I reminisce. Bad kids got "sent to the principal," and on a third or subsequent trip in any school year, the paddle was used. Clare Sorheim and Blub Stoneking tasted the paddle in our eighth-grade year. Blub was always fighting or picking on the girls, and Clare talked too much and at the wrong times. I did well in the classroom, curbed my impulse to interrupt and correct something or someone, and got along fine as long as everyone left me alone.

I couldn't get along with my so-called peers (*If they only knew*, thought I) down in the sweaty-floor gym playing basketball during physical education class. PE was Tuesday and Thursday, and we could bring slacks and change from our dresses for softball in the spring and basketball in wintertime. PE was mandatory for kids in grades seven through twelve, and there was no grade for PE. That was a good thing for me, or my straight-A run would have been smashed. I could hold my own at softball, because I was a good pitcher and could hit the ball once in a while. But I could not dribble. My breasts got in the way, and I got razzed unmercifully during basketball time. I didn't take it lying down,

43

and a couple of times one of my tormenters was the one lying down. So there I was, in Mr. Lunn's office for the third time, staring at the paddle while he stared through me. "You're the first girl to ever get the paddle," Clare had smirked at me as he left for home on that Friday afternoon and I took the long walk upstairs. In a scary sort of way, it did feel like an honor of sorts.

"Same old, same old, Judith?" Mr. Lunn had a small voice coming out of a small head on top of his tall, pear-shaped body. The last time I was up there someone had swiped a cartoon from my desk drawer and given it to him. In the funny papers, Li'l Abner was being overrun by Shmoos, little white, pear-shaped creatures, and I couldn't resist the comparison. Ernest W. Shmoo was clothed in a brown suit, armpit-stained, and Ernest W. Lunn was not amused. Now, here I was, and I was going to get it from yet another authority figure.

His soft voice continued. I guessed he was nice to everyone before he paddled them. "You know Mrs. Schultz is available to talk to, don't you, Judith? Maybe you need to talk to someone besides your own mother. It often helps when we're angry, they say."

"Yes, I know all that. Can we get on with it, please? I have papers to deliver, and my customers expect them right after school."

He half-turned to glance at the paddle over his shoulder; then he looked back at me in my school dress, his eyes as deep as the lake. "Run along and deliver your papers," was all he said, waving his hand sideways in dismissal. I did not run but strode, with my head high, down the two wide flights of stairs, superbly in control as usual.

The seventh- and eighth-grade classes went to a movie in Huron on the last day of school every year, and boys and girls paired up whenever they could. Danny Ray asked me to go with him. Me! "Is this some kind of trick?" was all I could say in reply.

He assured me that he liked me and wanted me to go with him, and so I did. He was probably the cutest boy in the whole room, slender with dark, wavy hair. He didn't pay my way, but he sat with me and offered me popcorn and caramels. I don't know what the movie was, only that the candy affected my remaining baby molar. When he put his arm around me and kissed my cheek, I knew I would always remember my first date, for it was there that I lost my last baby tooth.

Girl-talk was intended for my ears when we returned to the school's bathroom. "He asked everybody else." "I wouldn't go with him." "Doody said he was all hands." I didn't pay any attention and stalked past the gossipers. It was the beginning of the glorious summer of 1948, on the back of Danny Ray's blue Cushman scooter many days, a few kisses and no hands.

I was almost ignorant of the "hands" business when Father demanded in August that Mama take me to the doctor. "She hasn't had her period, has she? Well, have you?" He directed his first question to Mama, his second to me. I had to admit it had been Christmastime. My second trip to Dr. Heilsen's office in his Main Street home was even more embarrassing than the debacle with the bobby socks. But Father was mollified until a few months later— long after Danny Ray had quit me for someone else—when Father sent Mama and me to the doctor again.

There was no embarrassment this time. We barely got past the front door. "Mildred! Quit bringing that girl in here. She is intact and quite likely to stay that way, given her guardianship!" By now I knew the connection between the monthlies and babies, however murky the details. All the other girls chattered in the bathroom, seeming to brag about their "visitor" or "the curse."

"It's private," was all I would say when they quizzed me. And privately I began to wonder—did its absence have something to do with Mars?

Chapter 13

Father made me quit my paper route when I started high school. "You're too big a girl to be delivering papers," was all he said, but I was sure it was to deprive me of my spending money. He didn't whip me anymore; he only gave me the back of his hand for my smart mouth once in a while. In Iroquois, he began to also be cruel to Nancy, and I thought it was because of Daddy Bud's visit the first summer we were there.

Our biological father took both of us to Lake Poinsett, where his sisters had a big rambling house on the shore. They called it "the cabin." Grandma Bergie, their mother, was visiting from Detroit. She was a rawboned, already old Pennsylvania Dutch woman with arthritic hands like human claws. Daddy Bud, her pride and joy, was the youngest of her nine or ten children, and the only surviving boy. When we returned from the lake, matching brand-new bicycles were at our house, gifts for our June and July birthdays.

Yes, Nancy was getting it now because of Bud, I was sure. Once, Father hacked at her while carving a roast, because she reached too far across the table for a piece of bread. The knife split the flesh and skin half an inch between her index and middle finger. She should have had stitches, but he wouldn't let Mama take her to the doctor.

So I babysat for magazine money. Mr. Lee paid me twenty-five cents an hour to take care of his three babies while he and Rosemary went out drinking and dancing. They lived in a little farmhouse out by Aunt Helen's; I would stay the night, and he would take me home on Sunday morning. One morning, I didn't want to go home right away. I was out in an empty pasture at about noon, playing with the five-year-old, when I looked up to see Father already inside the fence and stomping toward me with mayhem in his every movement. Naturally, I tried to escape. He dragged me over the fence and laid my left underarm open on the barbed wire, leaving scars I will carry to my grave. "She is supposed to come home first thing in the morning," was all he said to the sputtering Lee couple when they asked why he didn't phone. I bled all over the upholstery in the old maroon, '38 Chevy, which had replaced the shiny green Ford when it gave up the ghost. Mama put ice on the wounds and then made butterfly bandages, for, of course, I couldn't go to the doctor for stitches.

Girls' glee club (there was no boys' glee club) met once a week with Mrs. Schultz and practiced songs it would sing for various school functions. "Where is Darlene?" she asked in late September, looking over the twenty girls in the room. When someone told her Darlene was absent that day, she called my name next. "I'd like you to sing this solo at the homecoming program," she said. The song was "If You Were the Only Girl in the World," and with Mama to accompany me, I practiced it every day. She was as proud as she had been of my selection as last year's homecoming princess, and as I did then, I kept mum about the truth. Making me princess was a cruel joke, and I was a second choice that paled beside the rendition that Darlene would have made of the hokey song. None of the congratulations I received that night changed my mind, either. Mama didn't come, of course.

47

Chapter 14

I had a real boyfriend, and he was a senior. He was well over six feet, handsome and rawboned with spiky red-blond hair that spoke to his Germanic heritage. On Wallflower Row at the homecoming dance, I was trying to find my I-don't-care place and couldn't, when he asked me to dance. I was no dancer—two left feet guided my size 8's—but he had a 1-2-3 style that was easy to fall in step with. In the previous year, when I was downstairs in Miss Ramsell's room, he had been going steady with a pretty blond senior girl with thick glasses, but she was gone away to work or school. "You sang that song real nice," he said to his new girlfriend choice, and that cemented our relationship, such as it was. A hamburger sandwich after the dance, a few cherry cokes after basketball games that winter—he was only the sixth man because Coach knew he smoked. He lived on a farm outside of town and didn't have a car, so parking and necking as the other kids did was usually out of the question.

At Christmas, Mama let me buy him a billfold, and he came to our house with two identical boxes. My present was an ornate "dresser set," quite the vogue in 1949–50, with a girly pink comb, brush and mirror inside the box. The other box? It was for my sister, and in it was a pink dresser set exactly like mine, with a slightly different design.

Fifteen or twenty red spots adorned my heavy breasts the first morning after Christmas vacation. "Better stop at Doctor's on your way to school," Mama said.

It was chicken pox. A freshman in high school and getting chicken pox! (I was to contract measles from my first kindergartener and bypass mumps altogether, common "childhood diseases" in the 1950s.) I was mortified, and I didn't feel sick. "Your brother and sister will have it in a couple of weeks," Dr.

48

Heilsen said. "I guess you got it from the Lee kids." I never knew they had it. Then came the final blow. "You have to stay away from school until the scabs have dropped off."

"A watched pot never boils," my grandma used to say. I wonder if she knew that a watched pox doesn't scab over and fall off. It was three weeks before I was back in my seat on the freshman side of study hall, *sans* any sign of chicken pox. In another couple of weeks, I was angered to see kids downstairs returning to school with scabs galore covering their little bodies. "Everybody who hasn't had it has been exposed," Mr. Lunn said when I complained.

My mama was talking to the priest when I came silently through the side door late one autumn day after school. I thought to sit at the kitchen table until he left, because I had nothing to say to a so-called man of God. "My Judy has the second-highest IQ ever recorded in South Dakota," she told him and quoted a number. The number meant nothing to me and was just another of her barefaced lies, I was certain. I cringed in shame for her, silent at the red chrome breakfast nook. (Thirty years later, when I wrote for those test results in order to bypass Mensa's half-day proctored exam, there it was, the same number. Mama, for once, had told the truth.)

Father didn't send me to the doctor anymore, but he kept strict track of my whereabouts. It was junior-senior prom time, and I would be the only freshman girl there. Mama came up with a long black-and-white checked skirt, and an afternoon on the clothesline drubbed the mothball smell from it. With a billowy white blouse and without my glasses, I looked almost pretty as I put on lipstick and ran downstairs to wait for my date and his borrowed car. "Twelve o'clock—no later!" Father admonished at nearly the last minute.

"Mama, please!" I pleaded for her intercession. "It isn't over until one, and then The Grill is staying open so we can go for burgers. Please, please!"

He had the last word. "Twelve o'clock, no later, or you

don't live here anymore."

All the doors were locked and my suitcase sat on the front porch at 2:00 a.m. I checked to see that there were clothes in it before I had the boy take me to another promgoer's house. I spent the weekend and went to school from there on Monday, but after school, her mother told me I couldn't stay there any longer. It was okay, for I already had another plan.

Just across the street lived a young woman with two preschool kids. She worked nights at The Grill, and I knew she had babysitter problems. Soon I had a bed on her enclosed porch, went to school days and took care of the children at night. It went on for three weeks. On Tuesday of the fourth week, I was called to the new principal's office.

The county sheriff was there. He had a runaway report on one Judith Mary Roberts, and he took me to De Smet to jail, over the principal's protests. "Send someone over to Jenny's," I called over my shoulder. "She doesn't have a phone. Tell her I won't be there after school."

Mrs. Sheriff was adamant, a round woman with three or four young children of her own. "You're not putting that girl in a cell!" So I slept on their couch and ate at their table for the two days until the traveling judge came to the Kingsbury County courthouse. Then the sheriff walked me over to the hearing, where Father intended to send me to reform school at Plankinton.

He was there, square and stiff with his suit coat on. Mama was red-eyed in her pink silk dress. The judge really wore a black robe, and a woman sat below, writing. I don't remember any preliminaries, just the judge saying, "And where did you find this runaway, Sheriff?"

"Er, ah," the sheriff mumbled. "She was in school, your honor."

The judge half-rose in his seat, sat down with a thump and said, "Please remove the child, Sheriff. I think I need to talk to these parents alone."

Nobody told me anything else, except the sheriff. "You're to go home with your folks," he instructed. "Don't stay anywhere else, or you will have to come back here." Father laid off me physically for the rest of my days in the home. Ink was mysteriously spilled on my school essays or on books I was reading, and my orange school sweater had to be retrieved from the stinking dirty-clothes repository in the basement more often. I still ran upstairs to vomit on occasion, his own Pavlov's dog, but I wore no more purple bruises. I felt the master of my own fate again, and I got cocky.

Chapter 15

I had to sell my Daddy Bud blue bike for school clothes. The boyfriend was away at business school, and I had no date for the homecoming dance, but I was supposed to sing from the bandstand. Frankie found me hiding in an alcove in the gym-become-dance hall. I confessed to him that I was scared to sing with a real band, and he reached into his inside coat pocket and said, "Here, this will help you."

"This" was a mickey, a half pint of a nameless blended bourbon. I took a big slug of it. There was no coughing, no sputtering, no reaction except the warm glow that began in the stomach, extended to my head and my toes and screamed "Send more!" I was instantly beautiful and became Kay Starr at the microphone. Frankie was my supplier, and he and the bourbon were pretty much my only friends in anno Domini 1950.

Father's carpet slippers were lying on the floor in the dining room when I came home from school one January day. I had just coughed up a precious half dollar to have my "it was lying around in the dining room" school sweater cleaned, and I didn't stop to think. I threw the offending slippers down with the dirty clothes. "Where's my slippers?" was the first thing I heard, all the way upstairs in my room. "Judy, get down here!" He was sitting on the cedar chest below the window, removing his Li'l Abner climbing boots.

Arrogance reigned. "They were lying around, so I threw them down the clothes chute."

His steel voice had that killer sound I had first heard when Keeto's arm was injured. If I knew what was good for me, I would retrieve them, and right now. Bravado gone, I went into the kitchen to go to the basement. Perhaps I wasn't moving fast enough, but for whatever reason, he shied the heavy boot at me. It lit at my feet at the corner of the kitchen counter. It was reflex alone that caused me to pick it up, for I was truly too frightened to have a conscious thought.

He was on me in four or five giant leaps, probably thinking I was going to throw the boot back at him. I think I screamed "You will *not!*" as I began to beat him about the head with the boot I held in my hand. A sliver from his glasses went into the side of his right eye, blood spurted, and Mama came running. He, of course, went to the doctor. I snatched up some clothes, called Frankie, and stayed with his folks for two days while I waited for an answer to my telegram and got ready to leave the plains.

"Wes has ousted me. Can I come to you?" was the total text of my telegram. Daddy Bud answered immediately and wired money for the train trip from Huron to Washington, DC. Mama came with all my clothes and a suitcase with no bricks, and she said she would take me to board the Dakota 400 the next day. She brought me a parcel with fried chicken and bread-and-butter sandwiches and cookies for the trip.

The Dakota 400 was a flyer, a train that had never been late a minute in its existence. It was forty-two degrees below zero when I boarded it in Huron. There was an unscheduled stop in Minnesota to repair a heating system, and then there was an accident at a crossing in Racine, Wisconsin. The Dakota 400 was late 1,300 minutes when it pulled into Chicago, where it was twenty-five below zero, and no accounting for windchill factor in those days.

The flyer that I was to transfer to was long gone, and my chicken parcel was long empty. A sailor from Huron—Daryl C. Thompson was his name—bought me a cup of coffee and kept a fraternal eye on me as I continued to check to see when I could resume the trip to DC. I tried to get up nerve enough to tell him I was hungry, but I didn't. After several hours, I got aboard what turned out to be a milk train—it didn't carry dairy products, but it did make many, many stops along the way. Of course, they were frantic at both ends of my route, but I was having a ball. A loving porter brought me a pillow and sneaked me a sandwich (today I suspect he paid for it himself) and told me to sleep; he would awaken me when it was time.

And so he did. In the Washington DC terminal, where they had monitored every train from Chicago for two days, were Daddy Bud and my childless stepmother, she of the pale red hair whom we called "Pinky." "Call your mother immediately!" were the first words I heard, harsh from the mouth of the dad I had not seen for another three years. "Where the hell have you been?"

Chapter 16

Montgomery Blair High School in Silver Spring, Maryland, was huge. It had stairs that went only up, and stairs that went only down. I spent half of my first days retreating from the down staircase when I wanted to ascend. I was only a sophomore but had been taking junior classes in South Dakota, so a schedule was arranged in which I still had the higher-grade math class and bookkeeping, and they filled in a junior class called something like "social studies," but that wasn't quite its title. Its teacher was a soft-spoken, bespectacled man who looked young to be a teacher, and I sat in a front seat so I could hear his soft voice better.

Bookkeeping students were juniors and seniors, many of whom soon wanted to be my friend. It didn't take me long to figure out they wanted to cheat from my work or ask me the answers, but I didn't care. They liked me. They all smoked, and I spent hours alone after school teaching myself to smoke Lucky Strikes without coughing and puking.

Phys ed was a graded class and met every day. I got my first B that grading period—volleyball, a game I'd never heard of before, was the chief undertaking in that time, and I was tall. I was furious at the B, not realizing that all my other phys ed grades would be C's. I kept a calendar, too, for girls were excused from showering when "their time" was upon them. I learned to say, "No shower, ma'am," exactly twenty-eight days from the last time I said it and thus had to make no explanations.

Manners were important at Montgomery Blair. I said, "Huh?" to my homeroom teacher only once. Thirty other voices singsonged, "Sir! We say 'sir' or we say 'ma'am!" as I cringed in my seat.

My social studies teacher announced to the class that he gave only one A, and that was to the new girl, Judith. I knew it was because he gave so many essay questions and tests, and I seemed to be able to write quite well. "Where's your homework?" one of the bookkeeping kids I wanted to hang out with asked me one afternoon as we crossed the footbridge on Sligo Creek. I told him that I forgot it in homeroom and would probably be in big trouble tomorrow, but I wasn't going back for it. Then I let him bum a cigarette. From that time on, I carried books and papers home with me, although I almost always got my work done in class or homeroom.

I learned how it was going to be at home in the Schuyler Road apartment on the first Friday. Pinky had told me I didn't have to ask for anything to snack on, to just go ahead and take it. So there I was when Daddy Bud got home before her and saw me with a chicken leg in my hand. He smacked me so hard it flew across the room, chicken drips marking its path across the hardwood floor. "We don't eat meat on Friday in this house," he yelled.

No one had told me that. I had no expectation that he ran his house, his wife, and now his daughter by fiat, until I discovered that no one went to mass, either. He didn't get out of bed in the morning until Pinky brought him coffee, put a lit cigarette in his mouth and placed a pair of clean white socks on his feet. A lovely woman, she was not allowed to wear makeup, and her blotchy redhead skin and pale eyelashes detracted from her beauty. Still, she adored him. I didn't care about lipstick, so it didn't bother me. I had to learn that noon was lunch and supper was dinner and not to leave even a book on my bed, or I would have to listen to him yell. So I spent my weekends wandering up and down shallow and beautiful Sligo Creek, seeking out sheltered spots to read my book and smoke my cigarettes. Daddy Bud and Pinky didn't drink, so I had no place to get bourbon until I got in thick with the bookkeeping kids.

Maureen pretended to be her mother when Pinky called to see if it was okay that I spend Friday night, go to the movies, and come home Saturday. Maureen's mother would pick us up at school, Pinky told my dad. Off we went, half a dozen seventeen-year-olds and me, with Maureen's folks gone for the weekend. I remember the woods—I think it was Rock Creek Park—and one of the boys, George, exhorting me to snap out of it and get with it. But my hymen remained intact, and I had the hangover to end all hangovers on Saturday. "We sat up most of the night," I lied to the parents. "Had a lot of fun just talking."

I skipped a lot of school and always was home to get the mailed notices before the folks got them. Maureen and I bopped downtown to the Kefauver crime hearings a couple of times. We weren't really interested in Kefauver or his fight against organized crime, only in flirting with the cute pages. I went to the Smithsonian one afternoon alone, and it fostered my fascination with all museums, great and small. It was one huge building with a tall, tall ceiling. Lindbergh's plane, the first to cross the Atlantic, hung from that ceiling. The chronicles of humanity resided in the Smithsonian, but, sadly, there was no record of otherworld beings.

Daddy Bud discovered my cigarettes, and all hell broke loose. "You'll not spend the allowance I give you for smoking," he yelled. They both smoked like chimneys and it seemed hypocritical, but I lied and said I wouldn't do it anymore. Every time I lied, I got a knot in my stomach: I hated my mama for lying, and now I was doing it.

My nice social studies teacher had a comment in front of the whole class: "Judith, the farther back in the room you sit, the worse your grades seem to become." I thought he was being mean, calling me out in front of everybody like that, and saw no other meaning in his remark. Classes were over for the summer after my second grading period at Blair, and I was glad. Daddy Bud expected straight A's, and my second card had only two A's on it.

Pinky got me a job. I wasn't yet fifteen and had to have a special dispensation, but soon I had a Social Security card and a summer job at her work, the International Brotherhood of Electrical Workers at Fifteenth and K Streets in downtown DC. I earned thirty-five dollars a week as a file clerk, and there were three other, older, high school summer workers. Pinky thought I was a little hefty, so she packed my lunch with half a sandwich, a pickle and a piece of fruit or two. It paid off, for I lost twelve pounds in the ten weeks I worked. Daddy Bud bought his first car in years, he said, about the sixth week after I handed over my paycheck each Friday. Would you believe, it was a green '39 Ford?

He wasn't home yet when Pinky sat me down at the table one day. I liked her a lot, and she wasn't mean even then, just firm in her decision. "Judith, I know you're still smoking. I want you to tell your dad that you want to go home, right now. Do that, and I won't tell him about your smoking again." I promised I wouldn't tell of our compromise, and now, over sixty years later, is my first recounting of the reason I returned to South Dakota.

Daddy Bud was startled but noncommittal. "I paid your way out here," he said. "Your other folks can pay your way back, and this time you are going to fly." When I suggested that my summer's earnings could pay for a plane ticket, he grew agitated. "That will be for school clothes!" and that was that.

I was welcome again in South Dakota, reservations were made, and we went clothes shopping. Flamboyant, Bud Roberts flashed a hundred-dollar bill and told the clerk, "School clothes. Let me know when it is gone." He had the last word on everything we bought, exactly a hundred dollars' worth, and I wondered if he thought I couldn't multiply ten weeks by thirty-five dollars. I took a size ten in skirts, thanks to Pinky's ministrations, and blouses and skirts were about all that worked for my top-heavy frame. But we did get a nice maroon two-piece suit to fit both parts of my anatomy.

I sat in the back of the big plane from Washington to Minneapolis. A pretty freckle-faced stewardess came back and sat with me. "First flight?" she asked me. When I indicated yes, that I was a little scared, she said, "It's my first, too, and so am I." In my naïveté, I believed her comforting words for about thirty years. She served me a fine noon meal and said, "We made it!" when I deplaned.

The Braniff plane from Minneapolis to Huron was a small two-engine cloud-hopper, and I threw up my magnificent lunch over North Dakota. The checkerboard fields below were fascinating, and I wished then and now that I had a picture of them. In mid-August, there were still some golden grains in the mile-square fields, interspersed with the blue of blooming flax and green alfalfa ready for its final cutting. Lush brown, freshly plowed earth squares prepared for winter wheat completed Mother Nature's patchwork quilt as we flew over the Dakotas. It was a sight to be remembered forever.

Even Father seemed glad to see me. They all met me at the airport, and on the way home we stopped at Cavour and had hamburger sandwiches and ice cream. He put a whole quarter under his plate for the waitress. Keeto had grown a bunch in these months, and Nancy was a quiet nearly teenager. Father said he wanted to talk to me when we got home, and I thought maybe he was going to say his sorries for being mean to me all those years. If he did, I was going to be sorry, too, for hurting his eye. But he had only a warning for me.

"Eggy reminded me of this," he said, "and I remember how they talked about that other girl when she went to her sister's for a year. They're going to gossip that you went away because you were pregnant," he continued, "and we know it's not so, so don't let it bother you."

59

Chapter 17

It didn't bother me a bit, but it must have bothered most of the boys. I got back to Iroquois High School with my new body in my new clothes, and they all wanted to date me. Dating, I learned, would be a soda, parking at the lake, and wrestling for my virginity. Frankie had graduated and married one of my former classmates, so I gave up boys until that first, spiky-haired boyfriend came home from boot camp in his USMC uniform. Oh, he was gorgeous. The Korean War was in full swing, and he was my excuse for not going out with other boys. We were promised, I said.

Editing the school newsletter for Mr. Horton was my only good time in my last school year. For the first time in recorded history, the Legion Auxiliary women did not choose the top student in the class to attend Girl's State. I had received a flash of insight the week before and knew it wasn't going to be me, but that poor excuse for precognition also told me it was to be Mary Kay, the second-best girl student. To give the old hags credit, they bypassed her also and went to the third-best student and an all-round good choice.

Then the marine's sister-in-law wrote him some gossip she had heard: his Judith was pregnant. She was showing his return letter to anyone who would look. "If Judith is pregnant," it was alleged that he wrote, "of course it is mine, and I will come right home and marry her." We had done nothing but kiss and hug in all our time together, and I was furious.

There I was: a pseudo-Martian alone and angry in the second six-weeks' period of English IV. We were in a workbook where we had to punctuate and correct the grammar of sentences and paragraphs, and that day's long paragraph referenced the *Spirit of Saint Louis*.

"Miss Larson," a boy asked the blond, bowlegged recent Huron College graduate who taught English, "what is the *Spirit of Saint Louis?*"

She hemmed a little, hawed a bit, and answered, "It's a painting."

Up went my hand, frantic in its desire to be seen. "Miss Larson. Miss Larson! It's not a painting. It's Lucky Lindbergh's plane that he crossed the Atlantic in. It's hanging up in the roof of the Smithsonian."

She was quiet but angry. "Judith Roberts, perhaps you'd like to teach the class?"

Over the years, I have manufactured scenarios to go with answers that I might have given. What I did say, however, was, "I could probably do a better job than you do."

She expelled me from the class, and I didn't care. *Grades be damned,* I said to myself. *I have valedictorian locked up. I only need three and a half English credits to graduate, and nine weeks of A's in this class should give me a C overall.*

The principal came to see Mama and Father after the evening meal, which I had just begun to call "supper" again. No one talked to me; no one told me of scholarships that would be available, of accolades yet to be had, or even of just doing the right thing. When they were through with their confab in the parlor, the principal told me that an "incomplete" got no grade, that I would have only three English credits and would not be allowed to graduate. "You have to come back to school and apologize to Miss Larson," he said. "It's your only choice."

Since I was so right, so rigid in my rightness, apology was not an option. Without school, life as I knew it was over at fifteen. Deserted by precognition, I had no forewarning of Betty Friedan, the God who appeared as if by magic in the Pledge of Allegiance or the demotion of Pluto. I was flying blind, unaware that the astounding size of *Horse Fair* at the Metropolitan would one day rock my world, or that I would have successful careers and know

61

great love. I settled. Shortly after my sixteenth birthday, in the maroon suit, I married an earthling.

~The End~

A Word from the Author

Confessions of a Martian Schoolgirl, while the grand prize winner in Reminisce Magazine's inaugural memoir book contest, is barely a novella, as you may have noticed! In order to present a reasonably sized book, I have added some of my favorite odd stories. Some are memoir, nonfiction from various times in the Martian schoolgirl's life. Others, classified as creative nonfiction, are flights of fancy on the nuggets of truth at their cores. The last two fiction pieces were created particularly for you and for this book. Enjoy!

J. R. Nakken
Tulalip, Washington
Summer 2015

~Other Odd Stories~

First Time

Memoir

The cool morning unfolds as she planned. Nebraska's Septembers are hot, and the old lady's vacant garage sits yards west of her cavernous tan house. It is filled now with the lingering warmth of yesterday afternoon. That heat shimmers on the dust motes and dances with them among piles of boxes, tools and discarded porch furniture. Her new hideout calls.

She never sees the old lady. Her stepfather goes above and pays the money for living in the basement, but she didn't think Mama ever talked to her. Her mother stays in the dark apartment with Little Sister all the time, because Father takes the car to work. Today she hopes those two women do not see or hear her as she circles the block while the school on the hill calls morning classes. Let the bell ring! She won't do the stupid stuff anymore.

The garage's main door isn't locked, but it's on the side closest to the house. She left it cracked a bit when she secreted the treasure yesterday afternoon, and now her five-year-old heart pounds as she scurries across the asphalt drive and around the corner through that door. Whew! A sneeze threatens at the dust she raises while removing a piece of carpet that covers the magic chaise.

Future stashes will include Lucky Strikes, Erskine Caldwell and Four Roses. Today, only *A Tale of Sandy* awaits her. A green apple, a piece of limp cheese and two of Sister's animal crackers are wrapped in wax paper next to the book. The tiny notebook from Hansen's Grocery waits, a yellow Ticonderoga pencil stub poking through the silver spirals at its top. She stretches, careful of the splintering wicker, and begins to read about Sandy's adventures.

It keeps her mind off school, reading does. But when she

65

stops to list a word she doesn't know—*littered, harnessed, greedy* —or to nibble a bit, the mad rises up and tastes ugly in the top of her throat. In this new town with its redbrick prison, they make her sit on the baby side of a partition, while the reading and arithmetic are all on the other side. When the mad turns purple in front of her eyes, she blinks and swallows and reads some more. It calms her; it is a good story, and she plans a trip to the Carnegie Library on Saturday to look up the words. She can't ask Mama; her mother gets really nervous about reading.

The noon bell rings. Mama will expect her home in ten minutes. She rubs her eyes beneath the patched silver-rimmed spectacles and tucks the notebook in the pocket of her jumper. *A Tale of Sandy* and the chaise are covered again, casually, with the dusty carpet. The young reader congratulates herself as she places her trash in an oily-smelling barrel just inside the door. She is going to ditch school every morning and thus will never have to color balloons in the dumb kindergarten ever again.

Siah, RIP

Memoir

She loved her cats and kittens more than she even liked me. In retrospect, I think it is entirely possible that my little sister felt the same way about me and my reading. I hid from my dysfunctional home with my nose in a book, except at the table, where reading was *verboten*. Nancy lavished her sweet heart on dogs and horses and cats. Especially cats.

I escaped the loveless prairie household before I was sixteen—left her and her feline friends to fend for themselves against the stepfather monster, our mother, the silent beauty, and a spoiled young half brother. Without a backward glance, I began an emancipated life and accumulated husbands, children and homes in several states. In none of those houses were animals welcome; none of those children were allowed to have pets. Especially cats.

A dozen years passed. Sister, her husband and their small daughter came from Idaho to relocate in Southern California. They stayed with us for a short time, the trailer with their possessions parked behind the house. It was three or four days before I realized my sister was making many trips out the rear door, sometimes with a dish held surreptitiously in front of her. The lightbulb flashed in my brain. A cat, of course.

"Nancy," I yelled. "Do you have a cat out in that trailer?"

She put on her best baby face; her eyes twinkled. "Sister," she cooed, "would I bring a cat to your house? A mother cat with several tiny kittens? Would I do such a thing?"

She was impossible to resist when she was teasing. "Well, I don't really care," I told her. "But they can't come in the house."

They soon had their own house, and the kittens were weaned. One Saturday, Nancy dressed her Shirley-Temple-look-alike daughter in the child's best Kate Greenaway frock and sent her out in the neighborhood with a basket of kittens …three of them, cute and roly-poly. Little Katherine returned an hour later. Four cute kittens now cuddled in the basket. My sister just chuckled. "The more, the merrier," she insisted, and she didn't try to give one to me.

Our paths diverged again, and another dozen years went by. Divorced and living in eastern Washington State, Nancy found her best friend. Rimrock's Siah of Beth-Al was a very spendy smoked black Persian with a pushed-in face. And *attitude*. Nancy's original idea was to make piles of money in the Very Spendy Kitten business, and to this end she took Siah to be bred when the regal Persian was of the proper age.

Rimrock's Siah of Beth-Al didn't care for the process. She didn't care for it at all and she protested at the top of her royal lungs. After a couple of extra days, the cattery gave up. Siah was not going to provide miniature push-faced dollar signs in this lifetime. Nancy didn't mind at all, gaga as she was over the black queen. She just had Siah spayed and continued to lavish attention and affection on her.

I was maturing and mellowing, although still a slow learner of the lessons of life. My children were teenagers, but there were no pets in my house. I remember being awestruck at a time when Nancy was temporarily without funds and had just enough coins for a pack of cigarettes. She returned from the store with a carton of cottage cheese for Siah, and a pack of gum. I vocalized my disgust at the time, but I can still call up the feeling of admiration that engulfed me at her selfless act. Oh, how she loved that cat.

Robert joined their twosome. His work took him around the West Coast, and the three of them—litter box and all—lived for weeks at a time in her old square Volkswagen van. They dreamed of buying property and settling down somewhere, and they actually took a sight-unseen option on some land near Bakersfield. Siah grew old and began to spend more and more time with the veterinarian.

My children grew and flourished and left home. I acquired a cat.

It was a fluke, a comedy of unbelievable errors and omissions, but I had a cat. He was a small brown Burmese with fur as soft as mink; his purr lulled me to sleep each night, and his rough tongue awakened me each morning. He turned up his nose at cottage cheese, but a month had not elapsed before I knew I would forego cigarettes to get it for him if he wanted it. Finally, I had a housemate who wouldn't leave me.

This was my altered state of mind when I opened Siah's death announcement that winter. Nancy's dear friend passed away while Robert was doing a job in Las Vegas. I lay my head on the desk and cried, the little handwritten card clutched in my fist. My poor sister. I didn't ever want to learn how terribly she grieved.

Nancy was determined to bury Siah on her own land, so they put the body on dry ice in a picnic cooler. It sat in the same place as the litter pan they no longer needed in the van, but it occupied more space in the cramped quarters. Robert's work in Las Vegas ended a few weeks after Siah's death. Robert, Nancy, Siah's dry-iced body and the van headed for California.

My scalp crawled when she called to tell me of the Bakersfield experience. "It was horrible, Seester," she said. "It was about twilight when we got there, and the land that was supposedly ours was moving. Moving, swaying back and forth, like a bad dream. The road ahead moved, too. It was huge spiders! Tarantulas, I think, and bazillions of them." Nancy refused to step out of the van and insisted that her husband forfeit the option monies.

Patient Robert was dedicated to my sister's happiness. Nancy's last words in that phone conversation were, "We're headed for Spokane. We'll bury Siah at Kitty's place." The Shirley Temple child was now an adult Jamie Lee Curtis look-alike with a home and a child of her own. The Volkswagen van, dry ice replenished, turned around to begin the long trip north to eastern

Washington. I gave CoCoa an extra tablespoon of treat for his dinner and more petting than usual when we retired that night.

If you are unfamiliar with Washington State, your immediate thought when you hear it mentioned is likely, *It rains all the time.* Then perhaps you think of lush ferns, beaches and forests of cedar and pine that soften the first wet image. This is only 50 percent correct. This description is of western Washington, from Puget Sound to the towering Cascade mountain range that divides the Evergreen State. Eastern Washington, while not devoid of its own evergreens, is a plain of contrast. Arid desert land and then the lush farmland of the gentle Palouse hills greet your eyes when you cross the wide Columbia, its ancient power dammed to all but the imagination. A stone's throw east of Spokane is the Idaho panhandle and the mountain passes that lead to Montana. Nestled between the two rocky heights, eastern Washington has sun and rain in equal proportions. It boasts fields of wheat in summer to boggle the mind, and stone houses, stone fences, stone walls. And it has clearly defined seasons ... hot summers, frigid winters, sweet springs and autumns that take your breath away.

It was February at Kitty's. Robert could not get a shovel into any of the frozen earth in her yard. Siah's final resting place was not going to be in Spokane, not that winter. "Robert has to go back to Vegas," my sister reported on the phone. Siah's beloved body had mummified in the ongoing weeks, and dry ice was no longer a necessity. "We'll find property somewhere," Nancy determined. She sent Robert off to the pawnshop.

They wrapped her with loving care, placed Rimrock's Siah of Beth-Al in the nice, nearly new suitcase Robert brought home and strapped it carefully to the back of the van. Discarding the cooler made the Volkswagen's interior seem roomy, after they had been living over and around it for so long. They took turns driving and just before dawn found themselves near Las Vegas. Robert pulled into a Denny's. Nancy patted Siah's suitcase as she passed by to go to breakfast.

The couple ate leisurely, speaking of areas where they could buy land and of the stone Nancy would paint for Siah's grave. When they returned to the parking lot, the unbroken lines of the Volkswagen's boxy rear greeted them, startling their joint imagination.

The suitcase was gone.

Smoke and Fire

Creative Nonfiction
The doorbell is chiming—ding-dong, ding-dong; slow and two-toned like that Avon commercial.

Remember when the Avon lady came every month? Her basket was full of scented samples, and she appreciated my order. These days one appears magically during the Christmas season. She hangs a couple of catalogs on my door in the middle of the night so she won't have to see me. If I want my soap or bath oil, I have to talk to her answering machine. She could be a man, a *nom de plume* on voice mail, for all I know.

The Avon lady brought tidbits of gossip from the neighborhood when she visited in the evening. "I'm not sure this is true," she'd titter as she placed yet another new product in my hands, "but where there's smoke, there's fire, you know." I wasn't acquainted with them, working all day and half the weekends as I did, but my neighbors' peccadilloes became familiar to me. And my mama used to say that, too. *Where there's smoke, there's fire.*

"What house does she live in?" I encouraged that the Avon lady's penchant for telling tales in suburbia, and I knew my neighbors only through her. The woman across the street in the blue house was in her seventh marriage. The two guys in the house on the corner weren't really uncle and nephew. You know what I mean. The redhead down the street had undergone four abortions. I knew them and remembered their sins, even when all had moved away and the Avon lady didn't come anymore.

Perhaps I should answer the door? Maybe it's a real Avon lady? I need soap.

The Company moved to Cleveland. I was highly marketable and took a position here that paid more than I'd been making at the other job after twenty-two years. I had a new staff o eight. Their sympathies were with their discharged supervisor, and two of them were deliberately making the work more difficult and my life miserable.

I called them into my office. "You have two weeks to get on the team," I told their two stone faces. "I could personally handle what you're both doing badly right now until I find other staff," I said.

"Yes, ma'am," they said.

The one who'd been there forever sat in her partitioned corner and smiled enigmatically, while the young one never came back. Our Workman's Compensation carrier had a claim within the week.

"Mental anguish. Sexual harassment. 'She rubbed against me and grabbed my chi-chi's,'" was on the copy of the handwritten claim form Personnel received.

I went to the insurance carrier's office and met with its attorney. They were negotiating a reasonable settlement, and my firm would have nothing to say about it. "It saves money in the long run," she said as she did not meet my eyes. We don't admit guilt, of course. She smiled and judged my crisp trousers, tweed blazer and the smoke in the file in front of her, and she did not offer her hand.

Photocopies of the claim and the payoff were on the windshield all the cars in the parking lot a week later. I still didn't know if chi-chi's were breasts or buttocks when the summons came from the State. The old girl continued to smirk in her corner. The new data operator shrank from me and ran to the bathroom, weeping.

The cat peeks around the corner. Does the doorbell disturb her? Should I answer it?

My new employer was allowed to bring the accused, an officer who could sign a settlement, and one other person to the hearing. This became the corporate attorney. "It makes more sense," I argued, "to take my ex-husband or current, occasional lover."

"It's too important," the president said, "to be without representation. The State takes sexual harassment seriously."

The accuser was allowed to present as many witnesses as time allowed. Still, she had only one. The bitter woman from the corner ensured her job forever by trembling in fear that I would terminate her for testifying. "No," she was finally induced to emote, "the new controller never touched me, but I was careful to keep a table between us at all times."

"I'm heterosexual, period," I said. "It's not feasible that I harassed this woman. Check my twenty-two years' work history. Talk to the last women I supervised."

Mr. Jefferson, the state arbitrator, heard me out and then ushered our party into a side room. We ventured small victory smiles. There was no proof; all we've lost is valuable time, our cautious expressions said. Jefferson came within minutes and asked for a check for $25,000 in full settlement.

"I'm guilty?" I asked.

"Without proof on either side, we choose to err on the side of the wronged," he replied.

Wronged? I could hear him thinking about smoke and fire as I collapsed.

I couldn't work anymore, even after I was well. Offices are full of women, and sometime I would have to be tough. So I garden and read and go to the movies—matinees, when the theater isn't crowded.

The bell stops ringing. The cat creeps out and laps at the spillage in the center of the room. It's not fitting, and I take her to my lap. The slut leaves her owner there and loves me immediately.

In the grocery, earlier, was a woman who lived across the street in the eighties. Everyone knew she had euthanized her mother in another city. Before I could consider what the real truth might be, she scuttled past me. I was ashamed.

I bought bullets for the thirty-year-old handgun. Three are

74

left.

The bell rings again. Ding-dong. A loud thump, thump batters at the door. I don't think it's the Avon lady.

Sarabande with the Slasher

Memoir

The sobs awakened her. Sniffles, as from one of the three young children conditioned not to leave their rooms in the middle of the night, had aroused her to a fugue state some unmeasured time ago. She was not maternal and began a return to complete oblivion then, but now she could not sleep for the uncontained weeping.

Her mouth was dry. Without movement, she began the panicky research that was her every awakening. No blanket protected her from Southern California's chill March night. As if shifting in her sleep, she tested a bare toe against her makeshift bed, passed a hand across a nylon-clad flank and inhaled a deep breath.

Good. Judith was oriented—clothed and on the tapestry couch in her own living room, its dusty peach odor of spilled Jungle Gardenia unmistakable. She continued to feign sleep for the benefit of whoever was crying.

It's Sunday night, she reasoned. Panic began to abate. *I don't have to go to work until daytime. Let me see, I packed up the jewelry and then ... No, wait. Oh, shit, I'm at the beach with the Greek.*

Memory assaulted her. The kaleidoscope that was Sunday afternoon and evening pounded at her temples and churned in her belly. Nausea threatened, and Judith wanted a drink. *Oh shit,* she thought again. *The no-class Greek. The no-class, no-balls Greek, and I missed the Santa Monica exit off the Harbor and got lost, and Albert had to stay here with the kids when he brought them home.*

Her gut cringed as she recalled her ex-husband's quie

words at the door. "You're ruining your life, Judith. I can't let you do that to these children."

The other woman hovered over her shoulder then. It listened to Judith's whispered scorn, calculated even in moments of extreme drunkenness to keep Mom and Dad's fights from the children. "You're going to take our little girl away from the brothers she adores? Sure you are, Albert, and then it will be you who ruins *her* life!" He was the only father her sons had ever known, and shame rushed at her then as she stood hipshot and disheveled in a fake leopard jacket and wobbly Springolators. Always she was ashamed when the Other Judith watched her, but still she screeched treats at the top of her whisper until Albert retreated through the front door, shaking his silvered head.

Judith's attention returned to the source of her awakened state. Either she was still drunk—and her desire for a shot told her she was not—or that wasn't one of the kids crying. Muffled, distinctly masculine moans came from the vicinity of her toes. *It's Milt*, she decided. The electrician she'd married briefly last year was a crying drunk and still had a key to the back door. *I need to get that from him*, thought Judith as she raised herself to one elbow and prepared to comfort the gentle man who loved her still.

Her long lashes parted. Light from the streetlamp on Norwalk Boulevard paled the heavy dark and outlined the large body kneeling at the end of the pink marble table. Dull sparkles tried to reflect from baubles along its length. *I thought I rolled it all*, was Judith's last thought before her narrowing life changed again and forever.

"Don't cry, honey. It's okay," she began. One fluid motion brought her to a seated position and sent her dominant left hand to Milt's bald skull. She patted and continued her croon until her fingertips' receptors translated the sensation of thick, curly hair.

It's not Milt, they shrieked.

Adrenaline surged, jerked her upright, and opened her eyes. The stranger flowed to his feet, and the black shape of his long body loomed against the shaded light of the dining room window. In the interminable seconds before either moved, Judith's senses recorded youth and rough work clothes, hooded eyes and heavy brows above a soft rag around the bottom of his face. She heard nothing, not even his breaths. He wasn't crying anymore.

Silent choreography began. Her feet slid two steps to the left, away from the coffee table that barred her escape through the living room door. The faint night light by the fireplace in the far kitchen area was peripheral in her expanding vision. The back door was there.

He matched her steps, countering to his right, and did not move otherwise. She heard a gulp or swallow, and then a long sigh. The soft sound electrified the fine hair on her arms.

A bare foot tangled in the Sarouk that covered a portion of the hardwood floor, causing her to stumble a fraction forward. He extended sleeved arms and pale, empty hands across the darkness between. Then, as terror claimed her and Halloween screams began of their own accord, Judith had a bizarre thought. *Shall we dance?* Her mind giggled while her vocal chords lamented, and her aberrant partner pounded through the dining room, kitchen and tiny family room and out the rear door.

Other Judith watched. *I didn't know you could scream like that,* it observed as Judith reacted. She walked the ten steps to the front door without taking a breath, flicked on the porch light, opened the doors mechanically and continued her shrieks while the intruder raced from the driveway at the right side of the house and disappeared onto the dark boulevard. One heavy paratrooper's boot was her final sight of his flight.

I've stopped screaming now, she noted as she ran to the black telephone on the dining table, its sheriff's and hospital phone numbers inked there by her own hand. *Good.* The dining room light came on at a touch, and her returning vision registered the open front door. Other Judith faded away, and she was now alone, terrified.

78

Judith ran to the door, slammed and bolted it, and then remembered the one the intruder had used. Her chilly feet flew across wood and tile and around the breakfast bar to the back door. It stood open to the night. She secured the knob lock and slumped against it, her heart threatening to throb from her throat. *Safe now, safe now,* her mind sang.

"I've had an intruder. Please come at once," she told the Norwalk Sheriff's Substation in her professional voice and fretted at the time it took to answer their dispassionate questions. While she waited, she thought of the Greek and his mass of curly hair. Oily hair, she remembered, and she raised her left hand to her nostrils. There was a faint odor of something like the boys' Brylcreem, and a brush across her cheek evoked a shudder with its suggestion of grease. She pawed through the stack of paper at the telephone for the man's business card.

"Yeah," he answered, obviously roused from sleep in his bed four freeways away. She could still see his stocky body with the love handles and matted black chest hair all the way to his groin, the deep, scabbed fingernail scratches on his back. She thought of the Metaxa she had spilled on his Danish modern coffee table. It probably still lay there, a sticky mess for someone to clean on Monday. Its thick brandy bile flavor rose now in her throat, and she could not speak.

Shivering with self-loathing, she hung up on his hellos and then jerked in returned terror as the instrument pealed against her hand.

"Hello. Hello!" The female voice tinkled in the air as Judith snaked the receiver up from the floor and sank into a red maple dining chair to answer it.

"Judith Reeves? You called about a prowler? Our car cannot find the address. Will you repeat it, please?"

So much for quick response was her thought as the dispatcher's apology tried to convince her it was Judith's fault the house numbers were transposed. Complaining toes sent her to the bedroom for bunny slippers while she waited for the sheriff's car, which was somewhere in her neighborhood. *They look funny with this red-and-black Kabuki outfit, but it's just cops coming.*

There were two of them, uniformed, polite as they stood in her living room. The younger one wrote on a clipboard while she told them what had happened and answered his questions. Yes, about ten minutes ago. No, I don't wear a watch. No, he was white. No, he wasn't stealing; he was crying, kneeling right there and sobbing. Yes, it was a rag, like a T-shirt. Well, it just felt like it. No, I didn't touch his mask; I just got that impression. No, I haven't checked to see if anything is missing. The jewelry? It's costume jewelry. I do party-plan demonstrations for extra income.

The other, fortyish deputy was rooted and silent. His eyes catalogued everything in the lighted living and dining rooms. They returned often to Judith, and she became uncomfortably aware of her voluptuous body in its lounging pajamas and incongruous pink slippers. "May we look at the rest of the house now?" Disdain and disbelief rang through the elder deputy's routine words.

One of the double-hung windows over the kitchen sink was fully open. "Look," she pointed. "That's how he got in. See, he stepped on the sink and over here to the breakfast bar and down." Her purse sat in its accustomed place on the bar, the red wallet partially exposed in its drawstring opening. The cops were murmuring to each other about attempted robbery and drug users.

"No, no!" She wanted them to understand about the haunted stranger with whom she'd shared the midnight dance. "Look! He stepped right over these prescription bottles." She pointed to the pills she took for allergies and premenstrual tension. "A user would have just scooped them up."

"And see?" she went on. "He must have seen the purse in the night light out here. Wouldn't he have taken the wallet?" She exposed the few dollars in its bill compartment as she spoke.

The young deputy didn't answer, still scratching facts on his clipboard. The other one returned from his quick tour of the

80

two tiny children's rooms and bathroom. "Your kids sure sleep sound," he said in a monotone as his narrow eyes appraised her again. "All that screaming and everything?"

Their house tour complete, the deputies returned to the living room. In their wake, she excused herself to the bathroom. She hadn't seen herself since she left the house at noon yesterday for a first brunch date with the moneyed man she'd met at a Long Beach club last weekend. Her bedroom eyes were mascara-smeared, the dark and teased hair tangled from sleep and worse, but she still looked good. *Older than thirty-one, though,* she told herself as she dried her hands and went back to face the minions of the law.

Clipboard was still at attention, but Unbeliever was slouched in her Victorian rocker, his cap on a crossed knee. "It could be a Metro walkaway," Clipboard argued feebly while he thumbed down through his records. Metropolitan State Hospital for the Insane was just a few miles straight down Norwalk Boulevard. "You remember, Chris? We had that call two nights ago? Just up the road? The woman who woke up to a man standing over her bed?"

"Did she say anything about crying, kid? Sobbing? Did we find any evidence of an intruder?" The seated man's sneer silenced his partner, who waited for his senior to finish the interview.

"So, what about this guy you called and found him home? Why did you call him?" The slit eyes didn't leave Judith, now seated across the room on the sofa. His russet hair was coarse, marked from the rim of his cap, and she imagined the stab of the stubble on the near side of his neck. Shuddering, she took a deep breath and was immediately sorry, for her breasts strained against the Kabuki jacket.

"Well, it was my first date with him this afternoon, and he did have curly hair and my address." Judith was not going to tell all. "And, well, he made a violent pass at me."

The seated man erupted and then interrogated her through

81

spasms of laughter. "Violent pass! Violent pass? What exactly does that mean, violent pass?"

She tried to explain. "Sorry, not really violent. Just a family joke between my sister and me. It just means, you know, like unwanted attention ..." She wondered if he was going to break the rocker before his roars subsided.

His young partner looked nervous and asked his first direct question since their return to the living room. "Can you think of anyone else it could possibly have been?"

She reiterated the fact that it was a sobbing stranger, and he tidied up his papers and made a move to the door. Senior partner sat unflinching in the fragile chair, cap on his knee and his weasel's eyes on Judith.

She stood and so did he, an eerie caricature of her earlier encounter that caused her to seat herself at once. He replaced his hat with exaggerated care and gestured at Judith and about the rooms.

"Tell me, Mrs. Reeves," he quizzed. "Is it your habit to lounge around in revealing outfits all the time?"

Clipboard interrupted from the open door, now anxious to extricate himself. "We'll turn the report in to the detectives," he announced. "You'll hear from them in a day or two." He leaned forward to hand her a card. His partner crossed the room and pretended not to hear Judith's astonished defenses—she was covered neck to ankle in a Kabuki jacket and pants, and every drape and blind in the house was drawn, and why did he ask that? He did not muffle his parting shot as she closed the door behind them.

"Violent pass, indeed! Now I've heard everything."

She told the children there had been a burglar and the policemen, our friends, had everything under control. All three were noncommittal as they ate cornflakes and packed their school lunches, their silent childhood insulating them from anything as remote as a nighttime robber. The office where she was so valuable

82

understood that she'd slept very little and would look for her at one o'clock. She pounded temporary nails into the kitchen windows, called the landlord to ask for immediate bars on them and a deadbolt on the back door, and tried to take a nap. Judith didn't drink on the weekdays and did not make an exception now, but she was glad that she didn't keep it in the house. Still trembling, she bathed and dressed in a tailored skirt, blouse, hose and heels to leave for her East Los Angeles job at noon.

Her first new car, a '65 Dodge demonstrator on which she'd carefully made thirty-four of thirty-six payments, sat in the single parking area behind the house. The registration, always to be visible on the steering column according to California law, lay ominously on the front seat. Its coiled wire frame was elongated, sprung when ripped from the post. Fear assailed her once more, and she went limp against the unlocked driver's door. The front door was bolted, she knew. Now she scurried back and tested the rear. Satisfied, Judith headed over to Washington Boulevard with the ravaged registration bobbling on the bench seat beside her.

"Yes, I'm the detective assigned to your case, Mrs. Reeves," the smoke-damaged voice on the phone answered. "Attempted robbery, it says here. We haven't gotten to it yet, of course ..." Judith could tell he was piqued that she'd called him so soon after the incident.

"No, sir," she pandered. "I'm just calling with more information," and she went on to tell him about the car registration. "He wasn't a thief, sir. He was crying, for God's sake. This is how he finds out if a single woman lives in the house." Judith was well informed about California's community property laws. Only a single woman had a car registered in her name alone. The detective interrupted her request that they take fingerprints.

"Says here 'attempted robbery,' ma'am. And we'll be looking into it the next day or two. Was there anything else?"

She lay her head on the desk and wanted a drink. A clerk came to the glass door and rapped, concern on her homely face.

Judith looked up and bequeathed a smile, waved her eloquent hands that everything was just fine and busied herself with the day's work. She took a circuitous route home that Monday evening, afraid to pass the temptation of her Friday night watering hole.

Judith slept little on Monday night. She paced the house, checked the doors and smoked many cigarettes, each new one lit from the tip of the last. She made it home by her new route on Tuesday to discover locks on the kitchen windows and a deadbolt on the back door. The crippled registration was again wired to the steering column of the locked Dodge behind her house, and her shakes were gone on Wednesday. She told the sitter to be extra careful and took her jewelry out to La Mirada for a successful party. The hostess served a champagne punch, which Judith declined.

She didn't expect to hear from detectives and was not surprised. By Thursday, she was reasonably calm and anxious for the weekend. The memory of the sobbing intruder was now relegated to the compartments of her mind where she kept the other chaos of her life. She skipped into the house after work that day, newspaper scooped up from the front yard, and started the rice dish the kids loved.

Judith scanned the back page of the paper while the skillet simmered. Bobby Kennedy would announce tomorrow if he was going to challenge President Johnson for the Democratic nomination. She read the whole article and then turned to the front page.

"Clues Sought in Death of Woman Here," she read. The partially clad body of a librarian, sexually assaulted and strangled on Wednesday night, had been discovered Thursday at noon. The librarian lived alone, it said, and the newspaper slid from Judith's paralyzed hands.

Her midnight dance partner had stopped crying and made up his mind. She knew it, as surely as she knew she needed a drink. She shut off the burner, grabbed her purse and called to the TV-glued children from outside the back door. "Going to the store. Back in a minute." She hurried to the car before the older boy insisted on accompanying her, drove straight to the Serene Room and started the weekend.

Judith called in sick early Friday morning and yelled at the kids for eating all the macaroons after their rice the previous night. When they were off to school, she phoned Martha. "I want to move out to Santa Fe Springs. Right now. I know it's mid-month, but we can find something. I'm coming out. Make coffee. No, no drinks. Let's find me a house first." Martha was her best friend, but you had to catch her early because she drank every day now.

It was an empty pink stucco tract house not more than half a mile from Martha's. They went back to Martha's kitchen to phone the number listed in the brown front yard. It was $175 a month, first and last, and fifty more than she paid for the little house she'd lived in for four years. She could move in tomorrow if her references checked out. "I'll probably take it; call you tomorrow," she told the eager owner, and she gave him her work reference and driver's license number.

They got pleasantly tipsy on Martha's endless pints of Ripple. Her friend talked against the move. "He's long gone, Judith. He'll never darken your door again, especially if he's the killer. The rent's too much. You'll have to get money from Milt just to move in, and you like your little house. And the kids should stay in their school."

Her courage returned with each pink glassful, and Judith grew determined not to be driven from her home. *I don't want to have to borrow from Milt, anyway,* she thought as she stopped at the Whittier Down liquor store for a pint of sour mash bourbon. *I'm staying home this weekend,* she excused herself. *I may want to fix a drink.*

The voice from above her shoulder reminded her: *You don't drink in front of the kids.* "Shut up," Judith breathed aloud. She turned into her driveway and consigned Other Judith to one of the last empty compartments.

Friday's paper had a follow-up story on the librarian's murder. It called the killer the Uptown Slasher, and there were no clues. Slasher? Judith marveled at the license used by the media. "Strangler" wasn't gory enough, she decided, and she went to call the sitter to say she was home early and wasn't going out again.

The bottle went under the pillow on her single bed. She started spaghetti sauce, put a load in the washer and thought of the drink she would fix when the kids were in bed. The three trooped in the back door, wary on Friday afternoon, and their delight in seeing her squeezed at her heart. *Shut up,* she thought at the silent voice. *Just shut up.*

She played Patterns with the boys, games she'd drawn on endless pieces of typing paper and given one of them for Christmas. The little girl wanted stories, stories and more stories and was soon asleep, grubby and smiling at her dreams. Endless minutes passed, and nine o'clock finally arrived.

"It's the Smothers Brothers, Mom. They're really, really funny. Can't we stay up until ten, please? There's no school tomorrow." She was warm with self-sacrifice as she acquiesced, reheated the coffee and picked up the book she'd been reading for weeks. Soon she was drawn into the television program by the boys' rollicking laughter.

These Smothers Brothers are hilarious, she observed. *Funny I never heard of them.* Somewhere between the skits about cougars in crevasses and whom Mama liked best, Judith made a decision. *I'm not going to drink anymore. I'm not going to drink even on the weekends. I used to read two or three books a week, for Chrissake, and never took a sick day. I wouldn't have to sell jewelry if it wasn't for my bar tab. I could spend more time with these good kids, who didn't ask to be brought into the world. And I could probably meet a nice, normal man.*

Her sons hugged her goodnight at ten o'clock and firmed

up Judith's resolve. *I'll give the jug to George and Martha,* she told herself as she went to the Dodge and put the unopened bottle into its trunk. *The kids and I will stay here and face the world. And now, I'm going to finish this book.* She read for an hour, moving from the sofa once to refill her coffee cup and put the last load in the dryer.

The knock didn't even startle her, although it had been months since Milt had paid a late-night visit. It was a staccato shave-and-a-haircut on the locked aluminum screen door. She lay the paperback facedown on the brown cushion, turned on the outside light and opened the solid wood door.

His clothes were different—a plaid shirt with white T-shirt showing at the throat—but she would know the eyes anywhere. A brown sack rustled and gurgled under his windbreaker, and the ruddy neck was shaved and raw. Judith was speechless as he stood in the overgrown yard and smirked.

"I know it's late, but I saw your light. I thought maybe I'd come by and try to make a violent pass at you," the deputy announced. He began to ascend the steps, self-confidence in every move.

"Go away," she breathed as she slammed and bolted the door. "Go away, or I'll call …I'll call …" She slid down the wall and slammed her hands against her ears.

Sometime after midnight, Judith Reeves went to the storage shed for the moving boxes and began to pack. On her second trip to the shed, she detoured to the trunk of the Dodge. Other Judith did not speak then, or again.

Flowers for Algernon's Grandmother

Memoir

I create happy stories to mollify my killer temper. Twice I attempted mayhem and worse before I turned my life around, and it was just a matter of time before I offed someone with the car or my little handgun. So I got rid of the Beretta and saw a shrink and practiced the anger management tricks he suggested a lot of years ago. But I invented the story idea myself and use it today, although I don't need it as frequently in this new millennium as I did in John and Jackie's thousand days.

Like this. A healthy six-footer races me to the checkout stand, perhaps actually clanging against my grocery cart. I was probably no match for him even before osteoarthritis and sciatica began their joint attack on the quality of my life. Do I stand behind his load of beer and sausages and seethe, raising my blood pressure with visions of what I'm going to have done to him? I do not.

His dog's just recovering from a lengthy illness, and he had to leave her in the car, I tell myself. He needs to get back to the parking lot *posthaste* and is so glad I didn't raise a fuss. I get warm with self-sacrifice and practice of the Golden Rule, and my heart rate stays at 62.

If a little red car raced past me on the right side and squeezed me nearly off the freeway entrance, did I run him down or even show him one of my educated fingers? (I use the past tense because cataracts have caused the cancellation of my driver's license and left me house- and garden-bound.) I did not.

His wife's about to give birth, and he's so grateful I moved over for him. He'll get to the hospital just in time to see his first child emerge and will never forget my kindness. Probably he will remember me in his prayers for many months.

They come to me out of the blue, these stories, and they make me happy.

Toward the end of summer, we went across the mountains to the daughter's for a weekend. At home, watering the garden and planters I'd nurtured since spring, we discovered two pots of New Guinea impatiens missing. They're dear to my heart, these flowers —which were seedlings and are now in the full essence of their Seattle summer beauty—and I was angry.

Some kid lifted them for his grandmother, I told myself immediately. She's even more housebound than I, and she was overjoyed to get the scarlet blooms in their clay pots from the grandson she doesn't often see. I even named him and was content with my make-believe.

Two weeks later, we were away overnight and returned to find a wooden planter full of impatiens and tall green spikes missing from the display under the hundred-foot maple in our secluded yard. It was the pride of my garden, and I cried and shook before I got back into the earlier tale.

"You ain't seen nuthin' yet, Grandma," was Algernon's response when she thanked him for the first two pots. "Wait until you see what I'm bringin' you next time!" I even managed a chuckle at the humor of my story's second chapter.

Last week I had my first cataract surgery, and I wasn't out of the house for five hours. A huge clay bowl of geraniums, lobelia and marigolds was missing from the upper deck when I returned. This third violation was so near the rooms where I eat and sleep and write that my anger was overlaid with fright, but fear was soon dispossessed.

"Please take the target chamber off your Ruger, dear," I instructed my husband. "Mount the cylinder with the magnums."

Algernon's grandmother had enough flowers.

Straight Little Piggies

Creative Nonfiction

I was closest to her, the youngest child and only daughter, although *close* is not an accurate modifier. We enjoyed a loving but guarded adult relationship in the last ten years of her life, a relationship of many giggles and few moments of real communication. My brothers are dry-eyed at this memorial service; time and logistics excised her from their upwardly mobile lives long before her death.

The dozens of her sober friends in attendance provide the tears. Most of those women, and a few of the men, weep unashamedly. The balance of the half-filled, satiny funeral parlor's occupants demonstrates emotion ranging from stoic to the snuffling away of incipient lamentation. Then there is I.

I was eleven when she quit drinking. Nineteen, when she tried to make the amends that I knew were dictated by her program of recovery. "I want to tell you how mortally sorry I am for the first years of your life," she began on that Saturday morning twenty years ago. Her big eyes were so serious, so filled with shame, that I wanted only to spare her.

"I don't remember any of it, Mama," I told her.

"Surely you remember an upside-down wastebasket instead of a seventh birthday cake? Or me not coming home the night you made your first dinner, tip-top tuna casserole?" She tried to forge ahead, and I cut her off.

"I don't remember, Mama. Anything. Only that I always loved you so much." The gratitude in those eyes was worth the price of the lie.

Of course, I remembered. I remembered the wastebasket with the one big candle on it—all in orange, her favorite color—when Michael had a big store-bought cake just two days before.

90

remembered four years later, trying to keep the casserole warm and finally taping a note on the pink wall oven and going to bed with only "It's good, Little Sis," as praise from two big brothers who would eat anything. Remember? I could still see the monster-movie face that greeted me when I came home from school the day after the tip-top tuna. One blackened cheek was impossibly swollen and covered her left eye; the top lip was split, blue and sticking out like on those African natives in the *National Geographic*. And I remembered everything in between—a succession of uncles and stepfathers, screams in the night, moving from the school I'd attended since kindergarten and having no friends in the fifth grade in our last neighborhood in Los Angeles County. I remembered staying in our rooms until 10:30 that last Christmas morning because she had a headache. Yes, I remembered.

How could I forget? Shoes. She had so many shoes. Spike-heeled, pointy-toed pumps and sling-backs with closed toes in a dozen colors littered her bedroom and bathroom floors, along with the little cloth and leather, no-soled booties she always wore when she wasn't in hose and heels. I had to wear black patent Mary Janes to the Sunday school my every-other-weekend dad insisted we attend, and the boys' good shoes were black wing tips. School shoes were always brown, with laces, so we knew in advance what was in the store for us on our semiannual trips for shoes. It was always brown sandals for everyday in the summertime; tennis shoes were only for school gyms, she affirmed.

I can still see her, an old newspaper on her nightgowned lap, one bootied foot curled under her butt and varicolored bottles of polish marching along the edge of the marble coffee table. They skirted the overflowing ashtray and the inevitable glass of amber liquid, stood at attention to minister to the half-dozen pairs of shoes beside her on the brown couch. In that last rented house, that fifth-grade neighborhood, she was home more than she worked and the rainbow of little bottles usually surrounded a can of beer. But, until the last scuffed months, she always polished the shoes.

There are precious memories of fun … precious few, but good memories. Bath time when I was little: she always sang, "This straight little piggy went to market," as she scrubbed my feet, wiggling each toe. Charades when I was older, when her seldom-heard laugh bounced off the walls and once she peed her pants; we all three dared to join her laughter as she ran to the bathroom. There were sing-alongs on the rare occasions when she sat at the piano. Always, at Christmas, we sang, "The Twelve Days of Christmas," all of us doing our special parts. "Five golden rings" was mine, and we laughed together each time Michael's tone-deaf "Two turtle doves" groaned from an unabashed pre-baritone. It was a quarter century ago, but my eyes still fill when I hear the song on the radio, and I wonder if the boys remember.

But mostly she screamed. She yelled at me and Danny, and beat Michael a lot with a shoe or whatever she could lay her hands on at the time. "You're the oldest. You have to set an example," was her high-decibel mantra. He was fourteen and six feet when he took a splintered piece of firewood from her hand and told her not to whip him anymore. Danny and I were shocked and silent as Mama went white and still, staring far away at her empty left hand. She left the house without a word, and we were extra-careful to mark her mood when she came home from work the next couple of days.

Our neighbors built a pool, which was the fourth or fifth in our Southern California tract. We were never invited to any of the others homes, but the lady had a Mom and Kids' day pool warming on a Saturday when I was nine. Mama was movie-star gorgeous in a lavender flowered bathing suit by Rose Marie Reid (why do I remember that?) and soft matching booties. She couldn't swim and she went into the shallow end only after lots of teasing by a couple of other mothers, who carried on even louder when Mama didn't remove her footwear. That was the first time I knew that all mothers didn't wear them, the booties.

It was a Sunday, to be the last Sunday in the fifth-grade house. She had an extra-big tantrum while Danny and I were getting ready for the Sunday school bus. "Where are your good shoes?" she screeched as she tore the closets apart, and she smacked us when we tried to tell her that we didn't go to the shoe store in January, that these school shoes were the only ones we had. Her eyes whirled like windmills in the black clouds of Saturday night's mascara; she was ugly-beautiful with her red mouth and straggly black hair, and it was the first time that I was really, truly afraid of her. Danny took my hand without a word when we got off the bus, and we stretched the half-block walk from the corner as long as we could.

The living room was a shambles. Every trunk and suitcase we possessed lay on the littered green carpet, a couple half-filled with books. Mama sat on the couch facing us. The drapes were open, such a rarity that I blinked at the infilling of California sunshine. It winked and sparkled diamond rainbows on the ringed hand that toasted a cup of coffee at us. "Pick a trunk. One trunk," she announced. "We can only take eleven hundred pounds on our four tickets." We were moving to Washington State, to Grandma's.

In retrospect, I realize it was her last hurrah, that train trip. She spent most of her time in the bar car, and Michael griped unceasingly when he had to go get money for us to eat in the dining car. I saw the new little diamond flower on her finger and even in the insulation of youth knew that she must have sold the big ring so we could take the trip, that it had paid for the new clothes and shoes we were all wearing. I wondered then if she was getting so drunk because she missed it; my dad had given it to her when they became engaged. The boys had to help her off the train and into the taxi to the bus station in Green River, Wyoming. Hours later, Michael left us in the back and moved as far to the front as he could get. Mama was screaming and crying, big tears I had never seen, as the bus navigated the scary switchbacks on the old Lewiston, Idaho, grade.

93

I don't think she ever drank again. Life was never peachy keen in Spokane; she still had giant mood swings the first few years, but she worked and tried to do mother-things when she wasn't doing something for her sober club. Michael left for the navy as soon as he could, Danny went on scholarship to college halfway across the nation, and Mama cried silently as she and I tried to sing "The Twelve Days of Christmas" alone.

I babysat a lot in my high school days. "That's not how it goes!" Five-year-old Amanda interrupted the song I was singing to her baby brother as I bathed him. "It's not 'straight little piggy.' It's just 'this little piggy went to market.' My mommy knows how to do it right!"

I wonder why I didn't see it then. The dots were all there, for even a sixteen-year-old to connect. I knew of her deprived childhood, with few clothes and no toys. I had seen the pain in her eyes whenever she had occasion to mention him, heard her self-deprecating chuckle as she said "my wicked stepfather." I knew with certainty that the mending rift between her and my grandma was due to her childhood days. And once she even told me. Almost —if I had been listening.

"Why did you stop drinking, Mama?" I asked her. We were putting me together before the prom, and she was warning me about riding with anyone who was using alcohol or any other drug. She stopped messing with my hair and stopped cold, and her eyes met mine in the mirror. They were a mile deep and wet as Lake Chelan.

"One day I woke up"—she tried to grin—"and my kids had only one pair of shoes."

I thought it was a joke, that she didn't want to talk about it. And besides, the left side of my hair was out of whack with the right. The moment flew away.

I left home right after high school and saw her rarely until I moved back here after the divorce. I wondered if going home to Mama was a never-ending genetic code, one that would be

94

repeated in a generation by my own daughters. Still, I didn't have a clue until I went to sit with her the day after I took the clothes.

"You may want these," the sweet-faced, gray-haired woman intoned. "We didn't need them." She pressed a plastic bag of black-and-teal booties into my hand. I went a little berserk, flinging off her kind arm as she tried to explain that the departeds didn't need shoes in the casket.

"My mama wants these! They go with her dress. No, no— I'll do it."

Thus it was that I saw my mother's feet for the first time in my life, and never in hers. Deformed big toes curled around gnarled, smaller brethren, resembling nothing so much as abandoned newborn mice. In that serene, satiny setting, I could feel the pinch of too-small shoes; my own toes curled in rebellion at the thought of the crushing, squeezing transformation of pliant childhood bones. I wept, and wept again in the shower at home, when I looked down at my much-despised size nine feet.

I don't know if Michael and Danny said anything to her before the attendants closed the casket. Maybe we would talk later. Now, I couldn't kiss her face, but I stroked one of the cold folded hands. "Thank you, Mama," I whispered. "Thank you for my straight little piggies."

Tomorrow, Santa Will Come

Creative Nonfiction
They'd call it child abuse today, he mused, dandling Keeto on his knee. Libby Anna, nearly five, knelt on the carpet between his feet. "You're gettin' too big for Grandpa to lug around, little girl," he told her when they begged for Indian stories. "Sit there, and I'll think of a Santa Claus story for you." Now he was doing just that ... thinking.

Nope, it'd be child abuse even to tell it. Imagine, Johnny and Lawrence—they were just kids themselves. About twenty-two, twenty-three. Nope, can't tell these little ones that story! He quickly improvised a holiday tale about himself, a little half-breed Indian boy on the snow-swept Montana plain near the end of the Great Depression. Manufactured ribbons and magic wings adorned Fanny, his old horse, and his tale had her aiding Santa when the reindeer got stuck—honest to goodness, kiddies!—in the ten-foot drift on the roof of the cabin that was home to him, his mom and dad and baby sisters.

He finished the story with a flourish. "When I woke up, I got the only thing I asked for, a Mickey Mouse watch! It was a fine present for a little Indian kid whose folks were poor. So I guess Santa was grateful that Fanny helped him out."

"What's 'poor,' Grampa?" asked Keeto, cuddling his pudgy neck into the old man's face. The piney odor of his daughter's enormous Christmas tree did not completely dispel the nostalgic fragrance of clean, warm baby. *Too soon replaced by grubby little boy,* he supposed.

"You know, Brother!" Libby Anna leaped up, arms akimbo "The kids that don't have toys. We give them to the marines, and they give them to the poor kids." She shook her ancient head at the ignorance of little brothers and said, "Is that all, Grampa? You takin' your nap now?"

Daughter bustled in the kitchen. It was her day off, and she wanted to make all the breads and cookies and puddings her mother had created, hoping to cook him a happy Christmas. He tried to tell her, a working girl, not to do all this, but she couldn't hear him. *She works herself mean, and everyone suffers*

He limped to the basement guest room. Keeto tagged behind, heavy-lidded. Daughter called after them, "Can he take his nap with you, Daddy?" They cuddled under the blue jacquard bedspread, a wizened brown man and small, shiny boy, soon asleep.

It was so cold, even under the covers of his bed in the corner of the big room. Papa Johnny had stuffed newspaper in the cracks, but the snow was as high as the cabin's three windows. You could feel its icy strength through the wall boards.

He didn't want to be in bed yet. It had been dark for hours, since Uncle Lawrence and Nante Elizabeth came in the sleigh. Last Christmas Eve, when he was only five, Santa didn't come until after the grown-ups were ready to go to bed. Tonight, he had already peed in the pot twice, he was so excited. It took so long, then so long again. But tonight was finally the night. Santa would come.

They were hogging all the warm from the woodstove, and only one lamp flickered. The four adults sat around the heat, laughing and drinking pop and whiskey. "Yeah, if I'da got a job in town like you girls' dad wanted me to, I'da been out of work in this dern Depression! Yep, ranch work will keep us in a roof and food until old Roosevelt starts his job in March! He'll turn it around; wait and see."

Uncle Lawrence talked a lot, laughed and joked even more. The little brown boy, big-eyed and silent, adored him from across the room. He sneaked up beside Uncle now, squirming in the crack

97

between him and Mama to toast first one side, then the other, making himself as small as possible. *He inhaled deeply; yeast bread was raising on the chiffonier where Mama kept linens and RFD mail and diapers and secrets. He had been warned away from its vicinity in no uncertain terms.*

Mama was nursing Baby Sister. The infant smacked and cooed and smacked again. Mama fed me like that too—she told me so. *He wanted the baby to be brown like him, when Mama and Papa Johnny brought her home from Grandma's. He cried when he lay his arm alongside hers in the cradle Johnny had carved from a lightning-struck cottonwood. His didn't look so little anymore, but he was still the only brown one in the whole family. He had sneaked into Mama's pretty powder box and puffed the sweet-smelling white stuff onto his face and arms. Papa Johnny licked him for it. Mama cried.*

He was warm and began to nod, slipping forward along Uncle Lawrence's left leg. "Little guy needs to go to bed and wait for Santa," Uncle said. "Here, I'll take him, Johnny. You go get the wood and see to the horses." Uncle smelled of chew and whiskey and long johns, and he didn't want to leave the man's strong arms. He held on as tightly as he could until Uncle rolled him loose and under the quilts in one motion.

"Santa's about due, little fella," Uncle announced.

Mama was buttoning up her waist, putting Baby Sister in the cradle. Then she and Nante Elizabeth and Uncle Lawrence were standing by his bed. He tried so hard to keep his eyes open. Mama's voice was high, funny-sounding. "I am certain I hear Santa Claus out there!" He jerked awake.

He heard something. Sleigh bells.

There they were again, closer. Was that someone on the roof? He was supposed to be asleep if it was. Then Nante was saying, "Look, look, at the window!"

Sleigh bells jangled once more in the silent night. White eyebrows, white beard, rosy cheeks—Santa was at the window.

98

Oh, oh, there were noises on the roof! He scrunched down into his pillow tick.

Uncle Lawrence was so loud. The boy heard him knock over the taking-off-boots stool to grab the shotgun beside the door. Papa Johnny kept it there in case a meal of sage hen wandered by. He opened his eyes in time to see the beloved uncle snap it shut and charge, bareheaded, into the white Montana night.

Bang. Bang. Two shots exploded.

He froze under his quilts. He had to pee again. Lifetimes passed before a solemn new Uncle Lawrence returned to the waiting cabin, slammed down the shotgun, spoke to the two women at the stove and the boy who cowered in the bed. "I got him," he announced proudly. "I got him."

"Santa, Santa." The old man stirred in his cold sleep and clutched the spread to his shoulders. He moaned aloud as the movement sent sharp pain to his hip. "Oh, Santa!"

Keeto awakened, knuckled his eyes and started to slide off the bed. His grandfather cried again, "Santa?"

"What'sa matter, Grampa? Don't worry, Grampa. Santa will come." The boy could hear his mother's voice upstairs, screaming at Sissy. He patted the brown face beside him and lay down again. Santa would come tomorrow.

The Last of the Sk'l'n'th

Fiction

"*C'm s'l N'v'r'l,*" Esther Simon breathed to the universe in her first tongue. "I am Butterfly," had been her morning mantra for more than nine decades. That prayer accomplished, she rolled her ancient bones to the edge of the bed and lifted the curtain's corner. Yes, someone was leaving her tiny backyard, heading to the waters of the bay and a boat on its rocky shore.

His retreat was nearly accomplished by the time her gnarled hand flung wide the rear door. "I know you, Jimmy Enterer," she yelled at the brown-sugar back. "Don't think I don't see you!" He was over the dune and gone before she closed the door. *Good-looking boy. He must be fifty or so now. Didn't I have a thing with his grandfather Ezra?* A picture teased at the edge of her memory, a picture of a handsome youth in full regalia holding her hand as they walked, as her dancing dress jingled. *Yes, a fine boy, but not of the* Sk'l'n'th. Imprinted for a millisecond, the colors were gone by the time she reached the teapot in the other room, the dancing couple's image up in smoke when she sat with her cup in the worn recliner and began to plan her day.

First, I'll see what Jimmy Enterer brought, and then I will take Them their treat. She waved both hands in supplication toward the east at the thought. *Flowers need to be trimmed, and Ruthie will be here for her language lesson after her lunch.* Esther's seamed brown face grew solemn as she pictured the granddaughter, expertly piloting that chair down the ramp from the big house. *Thirty now, and locked in the wheelchair for thirteen years. The last of our family.*

Morning sounds accompanied the dawn. The herons in the wetlands on the other side of Daughter's property screeched in multiple voices at an eagle trying to get at their nestlings. Jame

Nelson attempted to start his ugly old TD8 on the property adjoining hers. Chug, whang, chug. Esther imagined she could smell the diesel, see it polluting the old-growth cedar forest that encompassed half of their individual tribal allotments of land. *That man has no respect for his* N'k'l'm *grandfathers.*

Yes, there was another familiar morning sound: the ringing of an ax carried from Cap Island in the middle of the bay, his family's land these hundred years. Johnny Abrams—son of Jake, grandson of Emanuel—was carefully logging some more of his forest. *All the Abrams' gone now, most of them to drink, like Daughter's first husband, Ruthie's father. Me, Daughter, Ruthie and Johnny Abrams. The end of the Sk'l'n'th.*

Esther had been born on the reservation and had lived there all but the years at Indian school on the dusty South Dakota plains, but about all she knew of tribal history was that five coastal tribes amalgamated in 1887 to form this one reservation on choice Puget Sound. The Coastal Tribe obtained fine treaty rights for the ocean's bounty, and the Sk'l'n'th had only a handful of full-blood members left even then. Intermarriage and alcohol had taken the rest of them, and now four individuals, barren, remained.

The front door of her two-room cottage faced north, and as she stepped carefully over the threshold, Esther rubbed the whalebone with her right hand. Two giant orca ribs surrounded the door, greeting visitors in a silvery, seven-foot inverted *V. The orca, symbol of our people. Your whale, my whale, Matthew,* she thought. The sketch of a smile crossed her face as she remembered the museum folks who had insisted that those "relics" be preserved at their location. "My Matthew battled that whale for a full day, and those bones are mine," she had yelled at their retreating backs, brandishing a wooden spoon. *That was years ago, and they've never been back. Probably waiting for me to die.*

A white bucket sat at the stoop and advertised Ace Hardware in red. Jimmy Enterer's gift; it contained two inches of water and three small Dungeness crabs, two of them lethargic in the scant moisture. The third was attempting the impossible plastic climb. Scratch, scree, plop. It rested a moment and then tried again. Scratch, plop. *I do know about wanting to escape, little guy.* An involuntary shudder stirred her old bones as she remembered Indian school. *Long, hungry ride in a smelly train. School: hot, hot, no rain, scratchy clothes in the dust and no trees for shade. Cold, cold, snowdrifts taller than me, no heat. Whipped when I spoke my language. No supper when I put my head under the pump. Black-robed white men and women, never a smile. Dark, hot closet when I tried to get out the gate the second summer. Speaking my language only to myself, so I wouldn't forget. C'm s'l n'v'r'l. I am Butterfly.*

Around the corner at the edge of the forest, the Little People had been busy, surely to spare her back from the stooping labor. The marigolds and zinnias were expertly trimmed of all fading blooms; a neat pile of dull reds and rusty yellows adorned the flat stone path that surrounded the little log house. Esther hung her head in thanks and looked about for the balance. She glanced over her roof at the Big House looming over the water in its own log magnificence and detected nothing unusual. *It will turn up. It always does.*

The diesel odor was real now; James Nelson was busy scraping Mother Earth and muddying her waters to create his private boat dock. *Too lazy to haul his boat less than half a mile to the free tribal dock.* Last year he had begun to fell hundred-foot cedars at the water's edge for the same purpose, but on Esther's property. Daughter's second husband, with a rifle nearly as long as he was, halted the process until surveyors could get there. *Not bad for a white guy. Not bad at all.* This year, giant ferns and young blackberry bushes had all but healed the Earth's wounds.

There it was, the Little People's balancing. A Steller's jay blue no longer brilliant and darting eyes dull, lay on its side just into the forest's edge and near the covered dishes she took to Them each morning. *Life, death. Good, bad. Happy, sad. I guess it i their job. But maybe I would rather have stooped this old back a little more and snipped my own flowers?*

They will love some of this sweet crab. Esther hefted the bucket with an unwilling arm, tumbling the tireless crab onto its back. She sighed and lifted it from its prison, placing it in the rain barrel under the downspout. *Some should escape when they try so hard. Melvin can take it down to the beach when he comes to mow.* The bucket was lighter now; she faced the *V* of the bleached bones that surrounded her door, nodded in Matthew's honor and touched the worn gray spot with her right hand as she entered.

The water in the iron pot was boiling, and she dropped them in. "Thank you, Crab. Thank you, Crab," she intoned. Having promised Daughter she would not sit or lie down while the stove was operating, she stood at the window and gazed up at the Big House. It was three stories with a cedar slab roof and south legs twenty feet deep in the water—earthquake- and tsunami-proof, Daughter's husband bragged. A wide deck encircled the second, main floor on three sides of the log mansion, and a smaller balcony on the bay side served the bedrooms on the top floor. *Even a damn' elevator. Imagine! An elevator in a house. But I guess it's good now, for Ruthie can go up and down stairs if she wants to.*

Ruthie. She pictured Daughter's only child at birth, a pretty thing even in the midwife's hands. *Let me see—I was here in my house only two years when ...* and her mind wandered away from the beloved and only grandchild to the few weeks she had stayed in the Big House. She was only eighty-something then, but Daughter was insistent that she come. Daughter's husband was cordial, and Daughter herself went out of her way for Esther's comfort, but Ruthie at fifteen was Esther's only joy in the new log palace of thick carpets and four bathrooms. *If they hadn't built my little house, I would have escaped for sure.* Esther chuckled as she turned to her cooked crabs, gleeful at the image of her old body, stooped even then, trudging down the reservation road to freedom.

Ruthie. At fifteen she had been an amber, shining young

103

woman; teenaged awkwardness and angst passed her door with never a glance as she grew into the classic beauty of her Sk'l'n'th forebears. At sixteen, she won the Washington State diving championship in her class, and at seventeen she was in Florida with her Olympic trainer. A drunk driver on the beach ended her life as it was intended to unfold. She was misshapen, diapered, lacking her original beauty and paralyzed from the neck down today. *What wonderful thing did someone get, Little Folks, when that baby was struck down?* Esther shook her head at tears languishing in old, dry ducts and put her face into the steam as she grasped first one, and then two, cooked crabs with the silver tongs and lay them on the board to cool.

I'll lie down now. Funny how tired I get so soon. Take a nap before Ruthie comes. Take Them some of that nice, fresh crabmeat when I wake up. Esther lay on her star-centered quilt and closed her eyes. The rhythmic sound of Johnny Abrams's ax across the water lulled her to sleep. Nelson's TD8 was silent.

II

C'm s'l N'v'r'l. The whisper had barely cleared her lips when the pounding that awakened her ceased, whalebones rattled and her door slammed open. *Where is it? Where is it?* She scrabbled, sought and found the silent alarm button. From the edge of her bed, she confronted the intruder.

James Nelson stood there, as wide as the doorway, livid as a beached whale. "What have you done?" His scream shook the strands of green-striped pathos that hung from the pot in the kitchen window; his ham hands shook and rattled the bone he grasped. "I have stayed off your land, you old witch! I'm going to sue in tribal court." He took a step forward, his hands making a strangling motion while a growl issued from his throat. Just as he thought better of that idea and turned to go, there was a sound from the doorway.

Click. Click. Two barrels of Daughter's duck-hunting gun

104

were aimed at the belly that hung over James Nelson's green work pants, and the proud Sk'l'n'th face above it was Daughter in her ultimate glory. "You said what?" she demanded.

She was twenty years older than his forty-five and a woman on top of that, but James Nelson knew he had met his match in the double-barreled shotgun. He calmed his voice and tried to explain. "Now, Dora, I'm sorry I screamed and—"

"And what?" she demanded again. "And barged into a hundred-and-two-year-old woman's house to scare her to death? Well?"

"My cat is ruined. Ruined! It will cost thousands to fix it."

Dora lowered her weapon a bit and scratched the side of her face. "Cat? You have a cat worth thousands of dollars at the veterinarian?"

"My big tractor, the TD8 there in my woods. Someone has poured sugar in the diesel tank, and the engine is ruined. Who else could have done it?"

The Little People? Why would they? And where would they get a bunch of sugar? He's an ugly, mean ignoramus, but he's always been that. Someone else must have a grudge against him. But I'll check around for the balance, anyway.

Esther went to the sink to clean the crabs, for it was past the time she normally took the treat into the woods. Daughter herded Neighbor Nelson outside, talking a mile a minute. "I wouldn't stoop to such a thing, my husband is away on business, that *elder* in there can't walk through the woods to get to your property, and Ruthie's chair can't, either!"

Nelson mumbled a polite response. *Daughter must still have the gun on him.*

"I don't doubt there are many other people who don't like you, James. Go home."

Esther was filling a covered dish with barely seasoned crabmeat, and another with carefully pieced sections of fry bread, when Daughter came back through the open door. "He won't be

105

back, Momma. Are you okay? Do you need anything? Should I tell Ruthie not to come down?"

"Yes, no, and never, never, never, Daughter. That girl is the last of the Sk'l'n'th and the light of my life. I am just fine." Esther headed outside with her two little dishes, so Dora picked up her shotgun, shook her head and went back to the Big House.

III
Esther placed the crab treat carefully between the exposed roots of a giant cedar, taking her time to pick up yesterday's dishes in order to breathe in the forest's primal odor. All was clean and bright on this day; one sunbeam pierced the fragrant overhead canopy and made gemstones of a patch of morning dew. In her little clearing, she bent to sniff at a pink rose and then turned the corner of her house. A dish dropped, shattering the silence. Another few steps, nearly at the door now, the other dish crashed to the stones. Esther reached out for Matthew's whalebones and fell forever. C'm s'l N'v'r'l.

On the deck at the Big House, unencumbered by the pile of shapeless clothing at the foot of an abandoned wheelchair, stood a shining amber girl who leaped to the railing and swan dived into the bay. A Sk'l'n'th streak in the water, she headed for Cap Island and the ringing sound of an ax.

Retrograde

Fiction

Moans awakened her, complaints from a hoarse throat, unlike her own.

Her moans.

White, shiny and silver attacked her half-opened eyes, and she promptly closed them. Her giggle was inaudible. *Not the men's room at LAX this time.* Anything for a laugh when emerging from blackout. *Hospital for sure this time.*

Let me see. Santa Monica Boulevard PJ's. Trini is singing "If I Had a Hammer," too many times. One of the Bills brought me, and he loved the low-necked black jersey dress with the red rose meandering down its side. French 75's with a cognac shooter instead of gin. Did I get home?

Someone was there, there in the room. She attempted to move and heard a young voice. "Oh, you're awake, Leah! Lie still, and I'll be right back!" She had to lie still, she discovered, since she couldn't move her arms or legs.

Reverie encompassed her awakening senses once again. *Sandy Koufax hit a triple. He was about zero for a thousand when the fastball caromed off his bat and screamed into right field. They both spilled their paper cup beer laughing at the trainer chasing Koufax around the bases with the southpaw's jacket. Had to protect that $35,000 left elbow. Russell had a Medic Alert bracelet for contacts, of all things, and very little else going for him except love of the Dodgers. Very little.* She indulged again in a silent giggle. *Really little.*

Maybe I wasn't at PJ's?

Another female voice—older, authoritative. "Leah. Leah! Are you awake?" She didn't like its tone and refused to respond, allowing herself to fall back into the sweet cotton cloud and not even hearing the charge nurse's reprimand: "You must have been mistaken, Nurse Watkins."

"Pretty sure you're awake, Leah," the first voice whispered after a time and massaged her right wrist. "I can take these restraints off, Doctor said, when you're fully awake. Don't want you getting chafed." She smelled like lavender soap and continued to stroke and talk to her patient.

"Good thing you had an ID on you, Leah. We notified your husband, and he'll be here soon. He couldn't fly, they said, so he had to take the Amtrak."

Amtrak?

Husband? Have I been to Vegas?

Vegas. I haven't been there since Don Everly was speeding at the blackjack table, have I? I laughed so hard I spilled a chimney of crème de menthe and soda into the dealer's chips. Have I? The pit boss wasn't laughing, but he had the girl bring another drink when he closed down the table, just not a chimney.

What husband? The thoughts jarred her cotton-wool reverie, and she spoke aloud. "What husband?"

"I knew it! Leah, open your eyes and look at me. Leah!"

Busted. Leah Roberts opened her sticky eyes to the blurred vision of a pretty freckled redhead in white who continued to speak, now in a soothing tone. "Well, there you are. Look at you! Big green eyes all wide awake." Besides the 36-D's, Leah's eyes were her most remarkable feature, and she was pleased that the nurse-type appreciated them.

"Thanks. Where am I?" Her throat was dry, its usually mellifluous voice unremarkable, cracked. "I need a drink."

A bent glass tube appeared as if by magic, inserted itself into her mouth with the aid of a scented, freckled hand. *Water. I* smelled like a swimming pool, but she sucked at it nonetheless. "San Francisco General, Leah. You're a long way from home."

"Long way" is relative. Not far from Whittier, really, even by car. What am I doing here? Did Bill G. bring me to see the

108

Lakers and the Warriors? She relaxed and slipped into near-sleep again. *Oh, those Lakers. Hot rods for sure, and not just Hundley. Elgin, Jerry West ... good guys and great basketball players. What day is it? Does work know I'm in the hospital? In San Francisco?!*

"I believe you, Nurse Watkins, but she is obviously comatose again. Or at least sleeping. I will call Doctor Rehnquist. He wanted to see her immediately when she awoke."

The not-so-nice voice again. It tailed off as Leah pushed herself into slumber. *Joey and his horses. Joey, my last ex-husband. Wasn't he? The last? Was it he they notified? All the flowers in the infield at Hollywood Park, worth the trip and the heat and crowd in the paddock. Native Diver, the big black two-year-old. Joey didn't want me to bet him to win. Showed old Joey and his bitter vodka tonics.*

They jarred her awake, slapping her face while she was remembering Rosey Grier headlining at the sales meeting. *Didn't know the guy could sing. Champagne in real glass flutes, mounds of caviar and Rosey chasing the front receptionist and surprisingly, not Leah. Good party, good ...*

"Mrs. Anderson! Leah! Open your eyes now." She obeyed the authoritative male voice. His lab coat was pale green, and his glasses were old-fashioned, square and sitting on the end of his nose. "Fine, fine. That's good. I'm Doctor Rehnquist. You gave us quite a scare. You have been unconscious since your accident two days ago. How many fingers do you see?"

"Three." Voice still hoarse, she croaked at the nurse. "Need 'nother drink."

"Good, good," Rehnquist praised. "You're going to be just fine. Nurse, you can remove the restraints. Leah, we just wanted to be sure you didn't tear out the IV. Just a couple more questions now." Nurse Watkins fiddled with Leah's left arm and cautioned her not to move it, since the IV was still in. As the nurse moved around the bed, another man came into the room.

He was slight and silver-haired, walking carefully with a

knobby black cane. "I'm her husband," he told the two hospital staff. "George Anderson. I just got here from Spokane."

The doctor introduced himself as Nurse Watkins busied herself with the right arm restraints, and Leah's mouth gaped. "Husband? Who said? Why would I be married to you? Are you filthy rich?"

His eyes were black pools of compassion. "No, not at all. You say you adore me."

Her right arm tingled, and she began to raise it, to flex its fingers. "Who was the president before Obama?" Doctor Rehnquist continued.

The arm before her eyes was crepe-papery flesh; blue and distended veins traced paths across its hand, over and around brown liver spots. Reality slammed through her next thought.

They killed the president yesterday, and Jackie got blood all over her ...

Screams.

Her screams.

~The End~

Other Books by J. R. Nakken

Three Point Shot (For young adults)
Stream and Light: A Woman's Journey (Memoir)
Sweet Grass Season
Jacey Cameron in the Lost State of Franklin (For middle-grades)

~Publisher's Invitation~

As publisher of the nonprofit Preservation Foundation I invite you to visit us at our web site. While there you can read some of our 1,000 plus stories, enter one of our annual nonfiction writing contests, or find out how we can help you publish your own book.

If you wish to purchase more copies of this book or one of our other books you can buy them from us on our web site (which will help us publish other fine projects).

They are also available from Amazon and many other booksellers.

I hope you'll visit us soon.

Richard Loller

The Preservation Foundation, Inc.
www.storyhouse.org
preserve@storyhouse.org
615 889-2968

*"Preserving the extraordinary stories
of 'ordinary' people"*

Made in the USA
Columbia, SC
02 August 2017